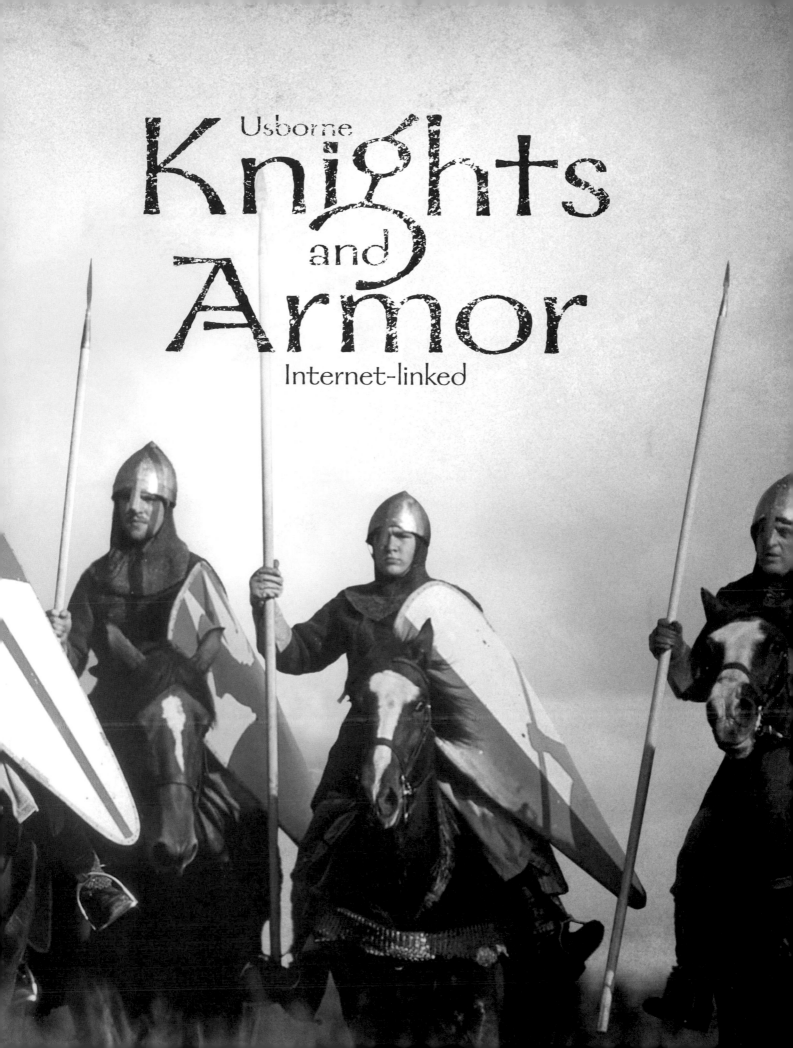

Usborne
Knights
and
Armor

Internet-linked

Usborne Knights and Armor

Internet-linked

Rachel Firth

Designed by Stephen Moncrieff

Illustrated by Giacinto Gaudenzi and Lee Montgomery

Consultants: Dr. Craig Taylor, Dr. Abigail Wheatley
and Robert Douglas Smith

Edited by Jane Chisholm

Additional material by Jane Bingham

Contents

Internet links

Throughout this book we have recommended websites where you can find out more about knights and armor, watch video clips, play games and test your knowledge with interactive quizzes. To visit the sites, go to the Usborne Quicklinks Website at **www.usborne-quicklinks.com** and enter the keywords "knights and armor".

How to use Usborne Quicklinks

Knights at war

Medieval armies

Most medieval armies were made up of soldiers on horseback, known as cavalry, and soldiers who fought on foot, known as infantry. Some foot soldiers were equipped with spears or bows, but for others it was each man for himself. They fought with anything they could get their hands on – axes, clubs, or even just basic farming implements.

Part-time soldiers

In theory, all troops were supposed to turn out to fight for their king or lord whenever he needed them. But the real story was rather different. Knights only had to fight for 40 days each year - and only at home, not abroad. Most foot soldiers and archers were farmers when they weren't fighting, and lords weren't supposed to ask them to fight during the busiest times of the farming year. This meant the 'fighting season' was usually limited to the three summer months, in between sowing and harvesting crops, when there wasn't much to do on the farm.

These foot soldiers are relatively well-protected. Many wouldn't have had any metal armour and would only have had very basic weapons.

Back-up team

Fighting troops were only part of the story. There were also huge numbers of supporters and camp followers who tagged along. Each knight had one or two trainee knights, known as squires, to attend to him, his horses and his kit. Teams of armourers and blacksmiths also had to be on hand, to mend damaged weapons and armour.

The people in this army camp are preparing for battle.

Servants help to put up tents.

This blacksmith is replacing the horse's shoe.

Draft dodging

Men who didn't turn out to fight faced heavy fines, but in England you could pay a fee, known as *scutage*, instead. The lord used the money to hire someone else. Gradually, more and more knights chose to keep out of danger by paying scutage. Many lords encouraged it, because it meant they could have their pick of better-trained, more experienced soldiers.

For a link to a website where you can find an online guide to knights and armour, go to www.usborne-quicklinks.com

This squire is helping his knight dress for battle.

37

1. Look for the "Internet links" boxes on the pages of this book. They contain descriptions of the websites you can visit.

2. In your computer's web browser, type the address **www.usborne-quicklinks.com**

3. At the Usborne Quicklinks Website, type the keywords for this book: "knights and armor".

4. Type the page number of the link you want to visit. When the link appears, click on it to go to the recommended site.

For a link to a website where you can find an online guide to knights and armor, go to **www.usborne-quicklinks.com**

Websites do occasionally close down and, when this happens, we will replace them with new links in Usborne Quicklinks. Sometimes we add extra links too, if we think they are useful. So when you visit Usborne Quicklinks, the links may be slightly different from those described in this book.

What you'll find

Here are some examples of the many things you can do on the websites recommended in this book:

- choose your horse and armor and take part in an online joust

- examine weapons and armor in online museums

- print out and make your own knight's helmet

- see if you can win the Battle of Hastings in an online game

- design your own coat of arms

- find a timeline of the First Crusade and play some games

What you need

All the websites described in this book can be accessed with a standard home computer and a web browser (the software that lets you look at information from the Internet). Some sites need extra programs (plug-ins) to play sound or show videos or animations. You can download these plug-ins for free from the Internet. If you go to a site and do not have the necessary plug-in, a message will come up on the screen. There is usually a button on the site that you can click on to download the plug-in. Alternatively, go to Usborne Quicklinks and click on "Net help". There, you will find links to download plug-ins.

Staying safe online

When using the Internet, please make sure you follow these guidelines:

- Ask permission from your parent or guardian before connecting to the Internet.

- Never tell anyone your full name, address or telephone number.

- If a website asks you to log in or register by typing your name or email address, ask an adult's permission first.

- If you receive an email from someone you don't know, don't reply to it - just delete it.

Note for adults - the websites described in this book are regularly reviewed and updated, but websites can change and Usborne Publishing is not responsible for any site other than its own. We recommend that children are supervised while on the Internet, that they do not use Internet chat rooms and that filtering software is used to block unsuitable material.

The age of knights

In Europe, over a thousand years ago - at a time known as the Middle Ages - there lived a powerful class of horse-riding warriors called knights. Knights waged war on behalf of their king and country, in the name of their religion, and to defend their own land and castles. Horses gave them huge advantages over other soldiers: extra height, speed and weight in battle. For over five hundred years, knights remained the elite force on the battlefields of Europe.

Metal heroes

Horses were an essential part of a knight's equipment, but his armor and weapons were just as important. Medieval knights wore armor that was stronger than any armor any warrior had ever worn before. By the end of the Middle Ages, knights were wearing metal armor that made them almost impossible to kill on the battlefield.

These men are wearing armor and carrying shields typical of English and French knights in the 11th century.

Lethal weapons

Knights fought mainly with swords and long spear-like weapons, called lances, and they developed devastating ways of using them. The invention of stirrups and new types of saddles enabled a knight to stay on his horse, even when he was dealing a heavy blow to an enemy. Knights also used shields to protect themselves, and the shield gradually became an important symbol of knighthood.

For a link to a website where you can take part in a joust (a type of fighting competition), go to www.usborne-quicklinks.com

This is an early 15th century Italian sword. Its long handle meant that it could be held with both hands to inflict a stronger blow.

8

Who could be a knight?

At first, any man could become a
knight - if he was brave and rich
enough. Kings picked their knights
from the men who were likely to be
the bravest and most loyal in battle -
qualities which were considered to be
'noble.' But, during the 12th and
13th centuries, knights were
increasingly chosen only from the
families of other knights.
Eventually, the families themselves
became known as
'the nobility.'

In this early 14th century picture, a knight is shown rescuing a lady from a wild man.
Stories of knights doing noble and brave deeds were very popular.

Knightly qualities

Even if being noble by birth qualified you to become a
knight, you were still expected to behave nobly too. Ideally,
this included protecting women, being merciful to enemy
knights in battle, and living by the rules of the Church.
These qualities were known as chivalry. How knights
behaved became so important that writers made rules
- or codes - for how the perfect knight should live.

Before knights

Horses were probably first tamed on the plains of central Asia over 5,000 years ago, but people didn't learn how to ride them until much later. Warriors on horseback have been around for nearly 3,000 years. The first ones we know about were a people known as the Scythians, who came from southern Russia. They were so successful in battle that warriors from other areas were encouraged to learn to ride too.

This Scythian comb is made from gold, and it's about 2,500 years old. It shows mounted Scythian warriors in battle.

The rise and fall of the Roman empire

About 2,000 years ago, much of Europe was controlled by the Romans, from Italy, who built a powerful empire that included parts of Africa and Asia. For hundreds of years, their power seemed invincible. But their empire was finally brought to its knees by mounted armies from central Asia. Between the years 370 and 450, the empire was continually under attack from ferocious armies of horse-riding warriors called Huns. The Romans were gradually weakened, and, by 475, their once-great empire had come to an end.

Hun warriors, like this one, were expert archers and used bows specially designed to be fired while on horseback.

Brave new world

The Roman empire had brought peace and unity but, when it ended, Europe was plunged into a period of chaos and instability, as rival warlords rose and fell from power. Mounted warriors were now in their element. As the once well-maintained Roman roads fell into disrepair, the only way to move around quickly was on horseback.

The Lombards, from eastern Europe, quickly took advantage of the situation and conquered much of southern Europe with the help of their mounted armies. In 774, they were finally defeated by Charlemagne (Charles the Great), king of a people called the Franks. Charlemagne had realized just how effective mounted soldiers were, and he created his own formidable fighting force of horsemen.

The paladins

Charlemagne recruited an elite band of horse-riding fighters, known as the paladins, to protect him and lead his troops in battle. They were ferocious warriors and soon gained a reputation for being particularly brutal. With their help, Charlemagne built a huge empire, which stretched from southern Italy to northern Germany, and lasted for almost 50 years.

Instead of rewarding the paladins with treasure, fine weapons and armor, as other warlords usually did, Charlemagne gave them land. In return, they had to promise to fight whenever they were needed and to remain loyal to him until death. This arrangement gradually caught on and was copied by other kings and lords throughout Europe for much of the Middle Ages.

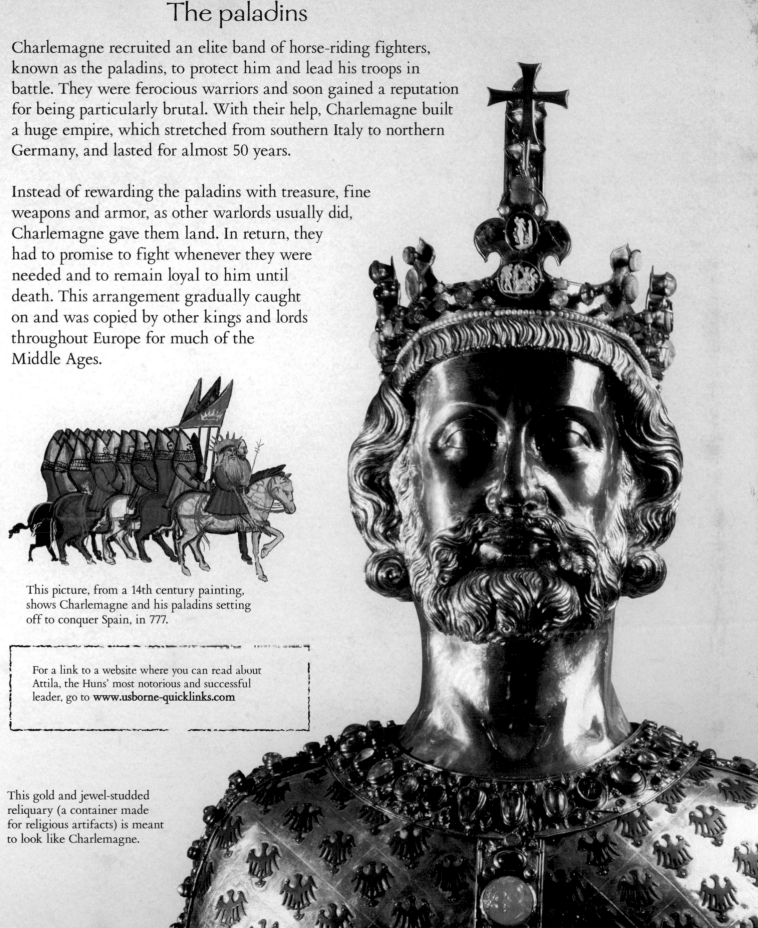

This picture, from a 14th century painting, shows Charlemagne and his paladins setting off to conquer Spain, in 777.

For a link to a website where you can read about Attila, the Huns' most notorious and successful leader, go to **www.usborne-quicklinks.com**

This gold and jewel-studded reliquary (a container made for religious artifacts) is meant to look like Charlemagne.

Life in the Middle Ages

In medieval times, also known as the Middle Ages, everyone had their place in society, with kings and nobles at the top of the pile, and people who worked the land, or peasants, right at the bottom. Some people call this the feudal system. But the way it worked varied from one place or time to another.

Kings and knights

Most noblemen, including the king, were knights - some were just more important than others. The king had the most power. He owned all the land, apart from what belonged to the Church, but he couldn't personally control every single bit of it. So, he entrusted large pieces of land to barons, the most powerful knights in the country. In return, the barons had to provide knights who would fight for the king for a set number of days each year.

This medieval picture shows the king who had ultimate control over almost everyone...

Lord of the manor

Barons divided up their land into smaller areas, known as manors, or *fiefs* (pronounced "fees"), which they gave to less powerful knights to manage. These knights had to swear loyalty to their overlord - the lord immediately above them - as well as to the king. They also took their turn guarding their overlord's castle, and promised to fight for him, and the king, whenever needed.

... and this one shows a knight going off to war to fight for his overlord - even though it means leaving his wife and child behind.

The peasants

Knights charged rent to all the peasants living and working on their land. The peasants paid in goods or labor or money, if they had any. Knights also demanded loyalty. In return, they promised to defend their tenants if they were attacked by enemy soldiers. Knights kept a tight reign on their peasants. Many were not allowed to move away from the land they lived on, or to work for anyone else. A knight could even stop his peasants from marrying, if he didn't approve.

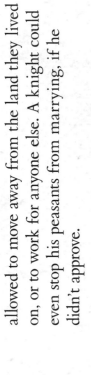
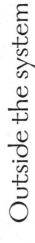

...and here you can see peasants working on land set aside for their lord - in return for being able to farm strips of land for themselves.

Misfit knights

Not all knights had their own manors. There simply wasn't always enough land to go around. Knights without land had to find other ways to make a living. Some collected taxes on local trade, or charged people to use certain roads. Others sold their services as soldiers, fighting for whoever offered to pay them the most. This made it possible for wealthy, rebellious knights to raise their own armies and wage private wars between one another - and even against the king.

Outside the system

In the later Middle Ages, more and more people started living in towns, and a powerful class of merchants arose outside the feudal system. Ordinary townspeople were able to buy their freedom and gain independence.

People who took religious vows, such as priests, monks and nuns, were also outside the system. Many worked for the nobility or the king but, ultimately, their loyalty was to the Pope, the head of the (Roman Catholic) Church.

Clergymen, like this one, had a huge influence. They could threaten people with hell after they died, if they didn't obey the Church's teachings.

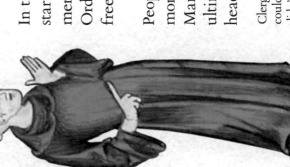

Battle gear

The main elements of a knight's battle gear - horses, lances, swords and protective body armor - didn't change throughout the Middle Ages. But new styles of armor and weapons were constantly being introduced, as technology developed and fashions changed. Battle gear was about more than just surviving in battle. It also became part of the very idea of what it was to be a knight.

Horse power

Aknight's horse was the most important, and the most expensive, part of his fighting kit. No one could become a knight unless he owned at least one. Most knights had several horses, bred for different uses. But the most valuable and expensive of all was the *destrier*, or warhorse. It had to be strong enough to carry a knight in armor, but agile enough to duck and weave in and out during battles.

This man is dressed as a 15th century knight, mounted, and ready for battle.

High-backed saddle to help the knight stay on the horse, leaving both hands free to fight

Cloth covering, called a *trapper*, to help protect the horse

Stirrup to enable the knight to grip the horse with his feet

Bridle

Reins to control the horse

Bred for war

Destriers weren't particularly large, compared to modern horses, but they were heavy, sturdy and strong. Their weight enabled knights to strike their enemies hard with a lance. All warhorses were stallions (males), specially trained to get used to the noise and chaos of the battlefield. Their training included learning battle tactics, such as the cavalry charge - which basically meant galloping headlong at the enemy at full speed.

Different horses

Knights' horses cost a lot to feed: they needed grain, as well as grass, to give them energy. They were also very expensive to buy, and warhorses were at the top of the price list. To protect their investment, knights only used their destriers for battles and tournaments. They had ordinary horses, or *palfreys*, to carry them around, packhorses for transporting heavy baggage, and swift, lean horses, called *coursers*, if they needed to get somewhere fast.

These are the different types of horses knights used.

Destrier

Palfrey

Packhorse

Courser

For a link to a website where you can find out more about medieval horses, go to **www.usborne-quicklinks.com**

Into battle

The battlefield was just as dangerous a place for a horse as for its rider. The enemy's main goal was to break up its opponent's cavalry charge. Not surprisingly, this often ended in injury or death for many horses. But warhorses were by no means defenseless. They could keep foot soldiers at bay by rearing up. Sometimes, they even wore armor. Horses were so precious that kings might offer knights insurance against losing their horses in war. This was known as a *regard*.

A sharp blow on the head from this rearing destrier would be enough to kill anyone who got in the way.

The enemy has placed stakes in the ground to break up the cavalry charge.

Archers stand at the ready to shoot down enemy soldiers once the charge has been broken.

Deadly weapons

Knights had a variety of lethal weapons at their disposal to use in hand-to-hand combat. The most important were lances and swords. Lances were long wooden poles with sharp, pointed metal heads, designed for thrusting. Swords varied from very long, heavy, double-edged, two-handed weapons, to much lighter, thinner blades with very sharp points.

Charging ahead

Before knights came on the scene, warriors used spears, designed for jabbing or throwing at their enemies. But spears had one major drawback. Once a spear had been thrown, it was often lost for good, as a mounted warrior couldn't easily pick it up again.

Lances were much heavier and stronger than spears, and weren't meant to be thrown. Instead, medieval knights tucked them firmly under their arms and then rode hard at the enemy. This was known as *couching*. Approaching at great speed, a knight could drive the point of his lance deep into his enemy's body.

Spears had to be thrown carefully. If the soldier missed his target, his enemy could pick up the spear and throw it back at him.

When a knight hit his enemy head on with a couched lance, it not only pierced armor. It could also force the enemy off his horse.

This spear has a barbed head, making it difficult to pull it out without causing terrible injuries.

The cone-shaped part on this lance, called a *vamplate*, is designed to protect the knight's hand.

Sword play

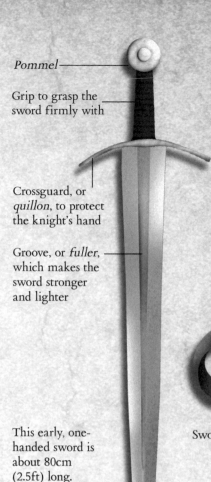

Pommel

Grip to grasp the sword firmly with

Crossguard, or *quillon*, to protect the knight's hand

Groove, or *fuller*, which makes the sword stronger and lighter

This early, one-handed sword is about 80cm (2.5ft) long.

Early swords had very sharp cutting edges, and they were designed to be used with one hand, while the knight held his shield in the other. As armor improved, shields were less important, so bigger, heavier swords became popular. The handles were long enough to grip with two hands, to inflict a more powerful blow. Blades also became narrower, and points sharper, so they could get between joints in armor.

A late medieval sword

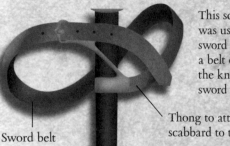

This scabbard (see left) was used for keeping a sword in. It was worn on a belt on the left hip, so the knight could draw his sword quickly.

Sword belt

Thong to attach the scabbard to the sword belt

Shaft made of wood, covered with leather

Metal tip, or *chape*, to reinforce the end of the scabbard

A 15th century French sword

Cut and thrust

Knights used the two sharp edges of the blade to swipe and cut, and the point to thrust and pierce. The weight of the sword was crucial for delivering crushing blows. A top quality sword could cut through chain mail and even metal helmets. To do this, it had to be immensely strong, but flexible, so that it didn't shatter on impact. This was difficult to achieve, so the best swords were extremely expensive, and highly valued.

This knight is about to deliver a crushing blow to his enemy. He uses two hands to give the blow extra force.

Here, the knight is using the point of his sword to pierce through a gap in his enemy's armor.

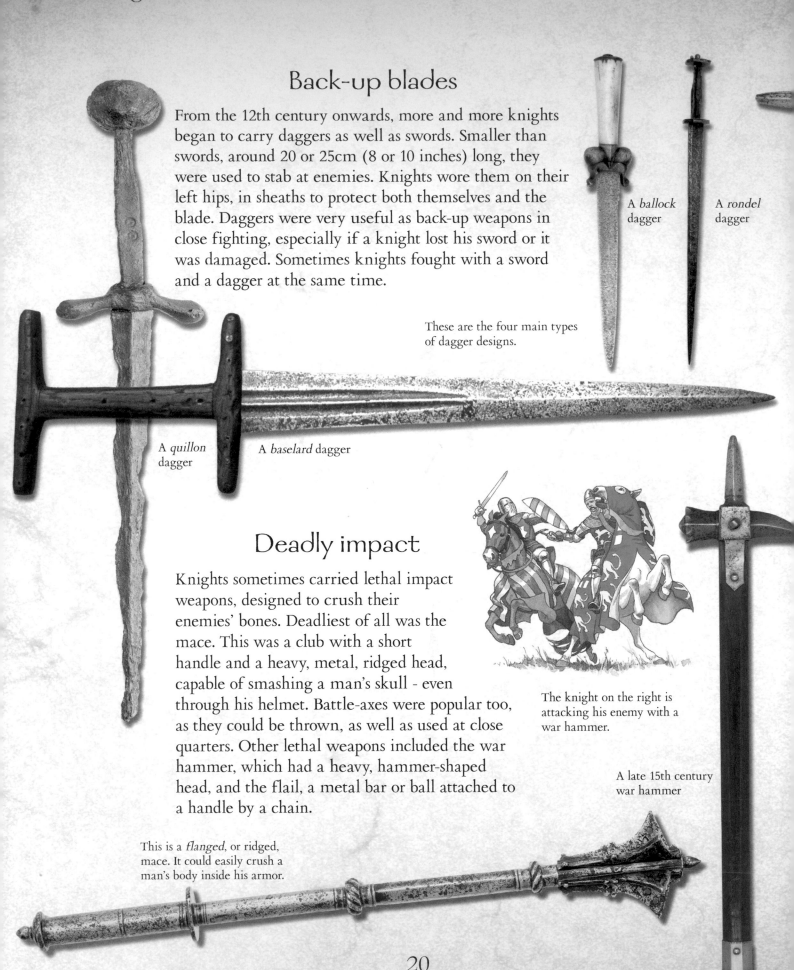

Back-up blades

From the 12th century onwards, more and more knights began to carry daggers as well as swords. Smaller than swords, around 20 or 25cm (8 or 10 inches) long, they were used to stab at enemies. Knights wore them on their left hips, in sheaths to protect both themselves and the blade. Daggers were very useful as back-up weapons in close fighting, especially if a knight lost his sword or it was damaged. Sometimes knights fought with a sword and a dagger at the same time.

A *ballock* dagger

A *rondel* dagger

These are the four main types of dagger designs.

A *quillon* dagger

A *baselard* dagger

Deadly impact

Knights sometimes carried lethal impact weapons, designed to crush their enemies' bones. Deadliest of all was the mace. This was a club with a short handle and a heavy, metal, ridged head, capable of smashing a man's skull - even through his helmet. Battle-axes were popular too, as they could be thrown, as well as used at close quarters. Other lethal weapons included the war hammer, which had a heavy, hammer-shaped head, and the flail, a metal bar or ball attached to a handle by a chain.

The knight on the right is attacking his enemy with a war hammer.

A late 15th century war hammer

This is a *flanged*, or ridged, mace. It could easily crush a man's body inside his armor.

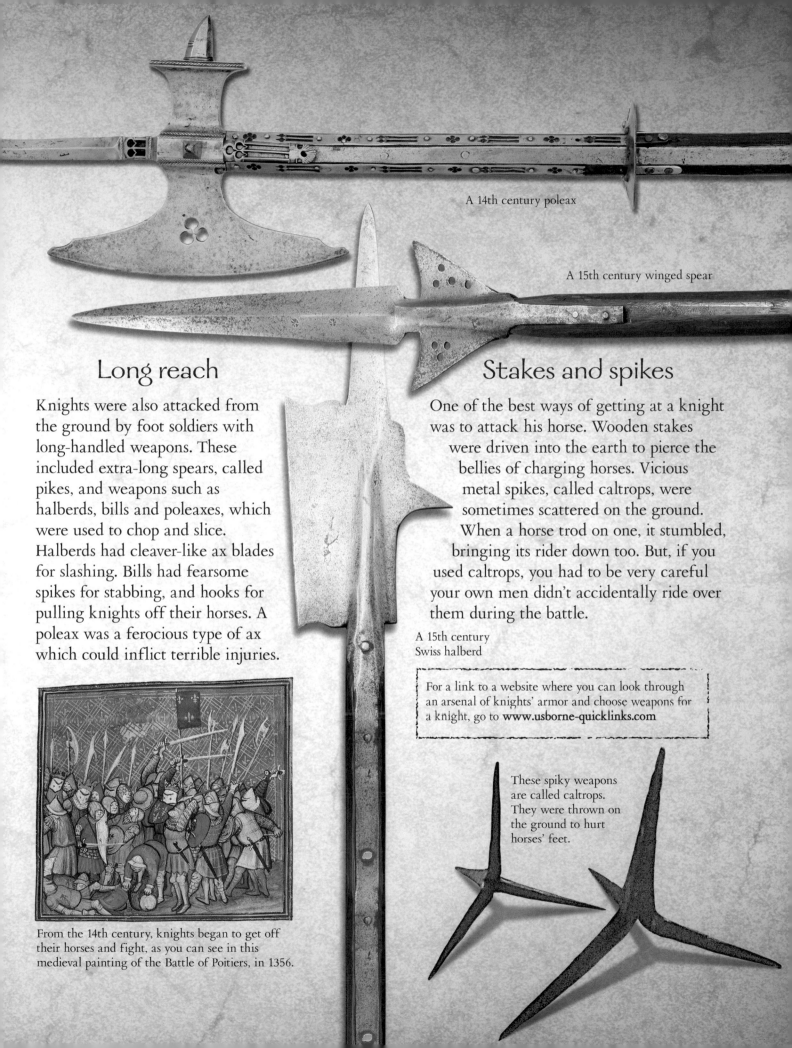

A 14th century poleax

A 15th century winged spear

Long reach

Knights were also attacked from the ground by foot soldiers with long-handled weapons. These included extra-long spears, called pikes, and weapons such as halberds, bills and poleaxes, which were used to chop and slice. Halberds had cleaver-like ax blades for slashing. Bills had fearsome spikes for stabbing, and hooks for pulling knights off their horses. A poleax was a ferocious type of ax which could inflict terrible injuries.

Stakes and spikes

One of the best ways of getting at a knight was to attack his horse. Wooden stakes were driven into the earth to pierce the bellies of charging horses. Vicious metal spikes, called caltrops, were sometimes scattered on the ground. When a horse trod on one, it stumbled, bringing its rider down too. But, if you used caltrops, you had to be very careful your own men didn't accidentally ride over them during the battle.

A 15th century
Swiss halberd

For a link to a website where you can look through an arsenal of knights' armor and choose weapons for a knight, go to **www.usborne-quicklinks.com**

From the 14th century, knights began to get off their horses and fight, as you can see in this medieval painting of the Battle of Poitiers, in 1356.

These spiky weapons are called caltrops. They were thrown on the ground to hurt horses' feet.

Bows and arrows

Knights didn't use bows and arrows in battle, but they were used against them very effectively. This made them a crucial part of the medieval armory. An onslaught by enemy archers could stop a cavalry charge in its tracks and knock knights off their horses before they even reached the front lines. The most basic type of bow was about 1m (3ft) long and had a range of about 90m (295ft). But the two most devastating bows were crossbows and longbows.

This foot soldier is aiming a crossbow to fire up above the heads of his fellow soldiers and into the enemy lines.

Crossbows

Crossbows, also known as *arbalests*, were widely used. They were particularly vicious and were hated and feared throughout the Middle Ages. Their arrows, or *bolts*, could drive their way right through any type of armor. If one hit you directly in the chest or head, you didn't stand a chance. They were also fairly easy to fire, so soldiers didn't need much training.

Hard to handle

Crossbows were very stiff. You couldn't bend their strings back to fire them just by hand. A crossbowman had to use the weight of his whole body, or a mechanical winder called a *windlass*, to pull back the string. All this took time, which meant you couldn't fire more than two arrows a minute. But, unlike other bows, you could wind the string back in advance so that it was ready to fire whenever you needed it.

The soldier winds the string back with a windlass.

Then he aims the bow and pulls the trigger to fire a bolt.

Longbows

The longbow was a bigger version of the basic short bow, and was used mainly by the Welsh and English. Longbows were difficult to fire and so you needed years of training to be able to use one. A longbow could be as tall as a man, and required great strength to pull it back. Even so, a skilled longbowman could fire arrows at a rate of 12 per minute. Longbows were not as powerful as crossbows, but they had a longer range. They played a crucial role in many English victories.

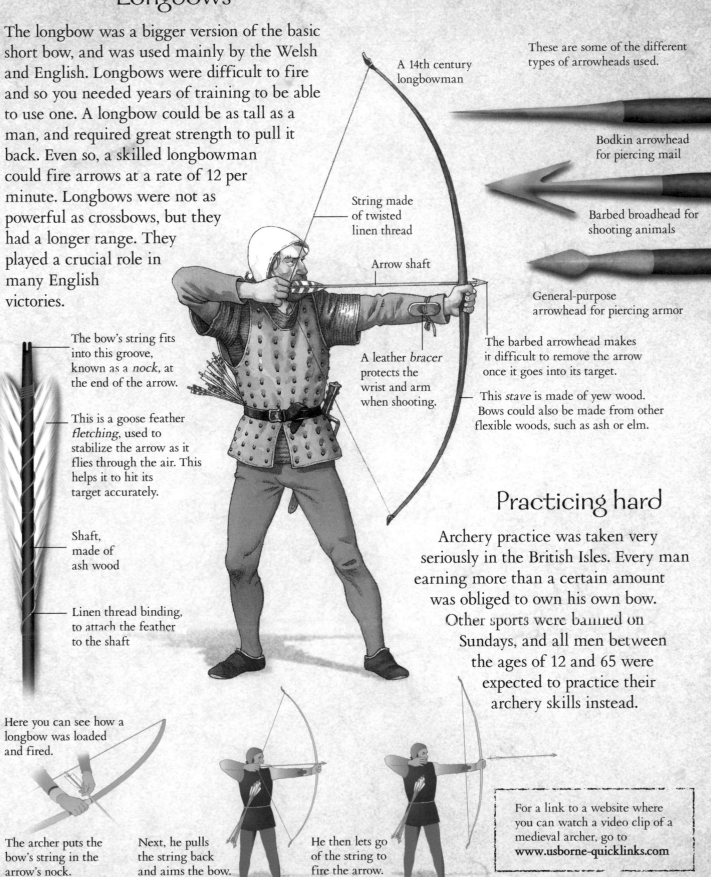

A 14th century longbowman

These are some of the different types of arrowheads used.

Bodkin arrowhead for piercing mail

Barbed broadhead for shooting animals

General-purpose arrowhead for piercing armor

String made of twisted linen thread

Arrow shaft

A leather *bracer* protects the wrist and arm when shooting.

The barbed arrowhead makes it difficult to remove the arrow once it goes into its target.

This *stave* is made of yew wood. Bows could also be made from other flexible woods, such as ash or elm.

The bow's string fits into this groove, known as a *nock*, at the end of the arrow.

This is a goose feather *fletching*, used to stabilize the arrow as it flies through the air. This helps it to hit its target accurately.

Shaft, made of ash wood

Linen thread binding, to attach the feather to the shaft

Practicing hard

Archery practice was taken very seriously in the British Isles. Every man earning more than a certain amount was obliged to own his own bow. Other sports were banned on Sundays, and all men between the ages of 12 and 65 were expected to practice their archery skills instead.

Here you can see how a longbow was loaded and fired.

The archer puts the bow's string in the arrow's nock.

Next, he pulls the string back and aims the bow.

He then lets go of the string to fire the arrow.

For a link to a website where you can watch a video clip of a medieval archer, go to **www.usborne-quicklinks.com**

Battle gear

A knight's armor

Armor changed constantly throughout the Middle Ages, to keep up with advances in weapons technology and changes in fashion. Body protection was vital if you wanted to survive a medieval battle. The most basic type was padded clothing that cushioned the knight from lighter cuts and blows. But, if he could afford it, he wore armor layered with metal for extra protection.

Chain mail

At the beginning of the period, many knights wore chain mail, which was made from thousands of tiny metal rings linked together. Chain mail gave good protection against glancing blows from swords. It was also very flexible, which meant that it could be made up into different shapes for tunics, hoods, mittens - and even shorts.

Weak links

Chain mail was very good at deflecting sword slashes, but it was less effective at protecting knights from lances and speeding arrows. Links tended to burst apart if they were hit head-on by pointed weapons. Chain mail didn't offer much protection from a crushing blow from a mace, which could break bones and cause internal bleeding. To increase their chances of survival, knights wore padded clothing under their armor.

The knight on the right is wearing a quilted undergarment, called a *gambeson*. It gives him extra protection, and makes chain mail more comfortable to wear.

— Hauberk

Aventail, to protect the neck

Ventail, to protect the face

This man's dressed as a 10th century soldier. He's wearing a chain mail tunic, or *hauberk*, with leather foot and leg protection.

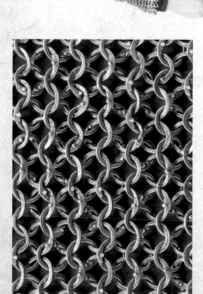

This is what chain mail looks like close up. It took about 30,000 of these links to make up a tunic.

Shield

Leather leg
protection, or *greaves*

Each ring was looped through
four other rings and fastened
shut with tiny rivets.

The rings were flattened,
and holes were punched
through its ends.

Ring

Warm wire was wound
around an iron bar and cut
into rings with a cold chisel.

Mail man

For a link to a website where you can
explore an online exhibition about
knights, then answer a quiz to dress a
knight in armor, go to
www.usborne-quicklinks.com

In the 11th century, most knights made do
with just a mail tunic, known as a *hauberk*,
and a mail hood, called a *coif*. Hauberks
came down below the thighs, and had a
split up the back and front to make riding
easier. They usually had long sleeves as well.
For extra protection, knights wore leather
stockings and thick trousers. By the 12th
century, mail was so popular that knights
were decked out in it from head to toe.

Hard work

As armor went, chain mail was pretty
high maintenance. It was made from
iron, which quickly rusted if it wasn't
taken care of properly. To rub off the
rust, a knight would get his servant to
scour the mail regularly with sand. It
was also very fiddly to make. This is
how it was probably done.

Suits of armor

By the 13th century, fashions were changing, and knights began to wear rigid breast and back plates as well as leg protectors on top of their chain mail. The earliest plates were made of hardened leather but, by the 14th century, this had been replaced by metal plates. Another hundred years later, knights were covered from head to toe in shining metal. A complete suit of plate armor was known as a *harness*.

Here you can see how the plate harness developed during the Middle Ages.

In the early 14th century, knights still wore mail hauberks.

A century later, mail was just used to protect gaps between plates.

This early 16th century knight is wearing a full plate harness.

Made-to-measure

Harnesses weighed about the same as chain mail. But they were much easier to wear, because the weight was distributed more evenly over the knight's body. The best suits were made-to-measure so that they fitted their owners perfectly. If you couldn't afford one of these, you could always buy a cheaper suit, ready-made in standard sizes, from shops, fairs and markets. Italy and Germany became the two most important centers in Europe for armor-making.

This is a 15th century suit of armor.

Bascinet helmet

Mail collar, or *aventail*, to protect the neck

Plate *pauldrons*, to protect the shoulders

Couter, to protect the elbow

Breastplate

Cuisse, or thigh armor

Poleyn, or knee guard

Metal shoe, called a *sabaton*

Showing off

Armor soon became important off the battlefield as well as on it. The huge cost of good quality harnesses turned them into status symbols. It became fashionable to wear very ornate armor, decorated with intricately etched patterns, often mimicking styles in ordinary clothing. Armorers also designed armor for special occasions, such as tournaments. 'Parade armor' was made entirely for show and didn't actually offer knights much protection at all.

This ornate 'Maximilian-style' armor, from Germany, was all the rage in the 1530s.

Upper cannon, to protect the upper arm

Couter, to protect the elbow

Lower cannon, to protect the lower arm

This is a finely etched late medieval parade helmet. It's shaped to look like an eagle.

Gauntlet, to protect the hand

Decorative fluting

'Wing' to give extra protection to the back of the knee

The end of armor

Back on the battlefield, plate armor gave knights the ultimate protection. Arrows and blows just bounced off it. But advances in armor-making were closely matched by developments in weapons. By the 1500s, there was a deadly new weapon on the scene: the gun. It was possible to make armor strong enough to withstand bullets, but it had to be very thick. This made it very heavy to wear. So knights gradually began to discard some of their armor and wear leather instead. The era of the knight in shining armor, galloping to war, was finally over.

This hinged greave protects the calf and ankle.

Helmets

A helmet protected the face, head and neck, which made it one of the most important parts of a knight's battle gear. The style and shape changed a lot over the years, as armorers developed better designs, and fashions came and went.

Slits to see through

Holes for ventilation

A 14th century English great helm

Early helmets

The earliest medieval helmets were small and pointed, made up of an iron framework with triangular iron sheets riveted to it. Cheek and nose guards were sometimes added for extra protection. These helmets became known as *spangenhelms* and were usually worn on top of chain mail hoods, or *coifs*.

This man is wearing a spangenhelm helmet with a nose guard.

Flat tops

During the 13th century, helmets had flat, or slightly pointed, tops and straight sides. This sort of helmet was called a *great helm*. It covered the whole face and had holes in it to allow the knight to see and breathe easily. Great helms were sometimes worn over the top of a rounded helmet, called a *bascinet*. A bascinet could also be worn on its own, depending on how much protection you wanted.

Padded extras

Great helms were heavy. To make the weight more bearable, knights wore thickly padded cloth caps, called arming caps, underneath. A knight could add a bascinet as well, to be on the safe side.

Here you can see the three different layers a knight could wear.

Arming cap   Bascinet   Great helm

All-around protection

Great helms worn with bascinets gave the knight excellent protection, but they were very heavy and restricted his movement. So, during the 14th century, a new type of bascinet, called a *great bascinet*, was invented. This was just as effective, but the difference was it could be worn on its own. A great bascinet had a hinged plate, known as a *visor*, that covered and protected the face. It could be removed altogether to let the knight see better.

This early 16th century great bascinet would have been used for fighting on foot.

Hinged visor with breathing holes

Steel plates to protect the neck

For a link to a website where you can watch video clips about armor and helmets, go to
www.usborne-quicklinks.com

Armets and sallets

In the late 15th century, a new type of helmet, called an *armet*, became popular all over Europe. Armets were made from a skull-shaped piece with added side pieces to cover the cheeks. These were on hinges so they could be opened.

Eye slit

Detachable hinged visor

This mid-15th century Italian armet would have been bolted onto a breastplate.

The *sallet* was another popular model at this time. It had a rounded skull piece that swept down over the neck at the back. Some sallets had hinged visors too. Soldiers sometimes wore a sallet with a metal plate, called a *bevor*, to protect the chin and neck.

A 15th century German sallet

The flared 'tail' on this sallet protects the neck.

This knight is carrying a heater shield (see opposite page).

Shields

For much of the Middle Ages, a shield was a vital part of a knight's kit. It protected him from spears, arrows and swords, and could be used to thrust aside weapons, and swipe at enemies and their horses. The shield eventually became the symbol of a knight's honor. A disgraced knight could have his shield taken away from him and hung upside down. Shields were also ideal for displaying coats of arms - the pictures and patterns that knights used to identify themselves in battle.

Shield design

The ideal shield had to be sturdy, but light, so it could be carried easily. Most shields were made of wood covered with leather, with a metal strip around the edge for extra strength. A short leather strap on the back, called an *enarmes*, allowed the knight to carry the shield on his left arm, leaving his right arm free to fight with. Another, longer strap, known as a *guige*, was for slinging the shield over his back.

If a knight was fighting, he'd hold his shield like this.

Guige

If he needed to use both hands to fight, he could wear his shield on his back.

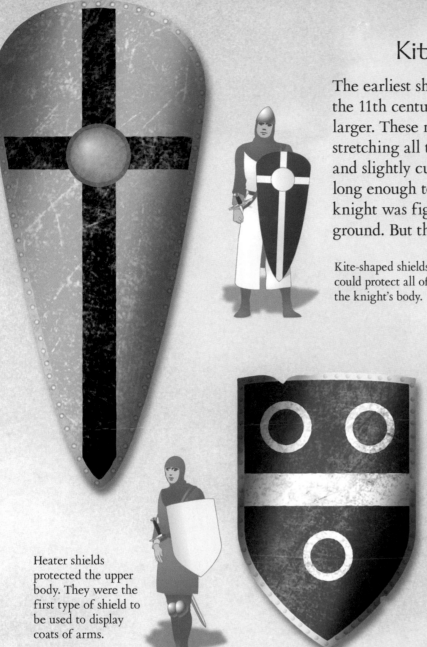

Kite-shaped shields

The earliest shields were large and round, but by the 11th century they were much longer and larger. These new shields were shaped like a kite, stretching all the way from the chin to the knees, and slightly curved, to hug the body. They were long enough to protect the legs – whether a knight was fighting on his horse or on the ground. But they were awkward to carry.

Kite-shaped shields could protect all of the knight's body.

Heater shields

As armor improved, knights no longer needed such long shields to protect their legs. So shields got shorter, which meant you could see over them more easily. By the end of the 13th century, knights were using small, light shields, which were much easier to carry. Pointed at the bottom, with a flat top, people call them heater shields, because the shape was similar to the base of a clothes iron.

Heater shields protected the upper body. They were the first type of shield to be used to display coats of arms.

Showpieces

In fighting competitions, called tournaments, knights used much fancier shields. They were smaller than shields used in real war, and often had a channel in the top, called a *bouche*, where the knight could rest his lance. By the 16th century, armor was so effective that no one used shields in battle anymore. But knights displayed them proudly in tournaments.

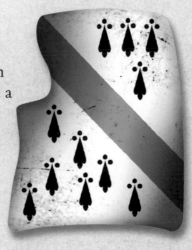

Tournament shields were permanently bolted to the knight's breastplate, protecting his left-hand side.

Horse armor

Whenever a knight faced danger, so did his faithful steed. From the 13th century, knights began to use specially designed armor for their horses. Horse armor gradually became more and more complicated, as it followed changing fashions, and it was always very expensive. Only the wealthiest knights could afford the latest kit for their four-footed friends.

This is a full suit of horse armor, known as a *bard*, made for a 15th century German king. There was a name for each part of the suit.

Crinet, to protect the horse's neck

Shaffron, to protect the face

Peytral, to protect the chest

Crupper, to protect the horse's flanks

Padding up

The simplest form of horse armor was a long covering of leather or padded cloth, known as a *trapper*. The trapper hung down almost to the horse's hoofs, but didn't cover the front legs. This allowed the horse to move freely. Really wealthy knights had chain mail trappers made for their horses, but they must have been very heavy.

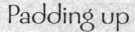

A trapper was made in two parts, one for the front and one for the back of the horse, with a gap in between for the saddle.

This very ornate horse armor belonged to the English king, Henry VIII.

Head gear

Sometimes horses wore extra protection, known as a *shaffron*, on their heads. Early shaffrons were made of hardened leather and covered the front of the horse's head, from forehead to muzzle. Later models were usually made of metal plates, and covered more of the head.

The full monty

By the 14th century, as horse armor designs improved, trappers disappeared. Shaffrons were often worn with a chest-protector, called a *peytral*, and sometimes with side and rear protectors, known as *flanchards* and *cruppers*. The early versions were made of hardened leather, but they were replaced by metal plates.

Knights at war

Throughout the Middle Ages, there was always a war being fought somewhere. It could be anything from a short-lived skirmish between rival nobles, to a full-scale war between kings. Wars could drag on for decades. If there weren't any at home, knights often went off to fight in someone else's war. This gave them valuable experience on the battlefield and kept their fighting skills up to par.

Medieval armies

Most medieval armies were made up of soldiers on horseback, known as cavalry, and soldiers who fought on foot, known as infantry. Some foot soldiers were equipped with spears or bows, but for others it was each man for himself. They fought with anything they could get their hands on – axes, clubs, or even just basic farming implements.

Part-time soldiers

In theory, all troops were supposed to show up to fight for their king or lord whenever he needed them. But the real story was rather different. Knights only had to fight for 40 days each year - and only at home, not overseas. Most foot soldiers and archers were farmers when they weren't fighting, and lords weren't supposed to ask them to fight during the busiest times of the farming year. This meant the 'fighting season' was usually limited to the three summer months, in between sowing and harvesting crops, when there wasn't much to do on the farm.

These foot soldiers are relatively well-protected. Many wouldn't have had any metal armor and would only have had very basic weapons.

Back-up team

Fighting troops were only part of the story. There were also huge numbers of supporters and camp followers who tagged along. Each knight had one or two trainee knights, known as squires, to attend to him, his horses and his kit. Teams of armorers and blacksmiths also had to be on hand, to mend damaged weapons and armor.

The people in this army camp are preparing for battle.

Servants help to put up tents.

This blacksmith is replacing the horse's shoe.

Draft dodging

Men who didn't turn out to fight faced heavy fines, but in England you could pay a fee, known as *scutage*, instead. The lord used the money to hire someone else. Gradually, more and more knights chose to keep out of danger by paying scutage. Many lords encouraged it, because it meant they could have their pick of better-trained, more experienced soldiers.

For a link to a website where you can find an online guide to knights and armor, go to
www.usborne-quicklinks.com

This squire is helping his knight dress for battle.

Battle tactics

Medieval battles must have been extremely noisy and very confusing - with the clashing of weapons and armor, the thundering of horses' hoofs, and arrows whizzing everywhere. To succeed in battle depended on having well thought-out tactics, a really good battle plan and, of course, very tight discipline.

Charge!

For a link to a website where you can play a game to reenact the Battle of Hastings, go to **www.usborne-quicklinks.com**

At the height of the Middle Ages, the most devastating battle tactic was the cavalry charge. When used really well, it could decide the result of the entire battle. Knights arranged their horses in a tight line and galloped at the enemy, with their lances firmly couched under their arms. This could shatter the enemy's front line of foot soldiers - provided they weren't packed too tightly - and break up the ranks of enemy knights by knocking them off their horses. The only problem was if they couldn't break through enemy lines. Then they could be thrown back, and end up trampling down their own troops.

These knights are lined up ready to charge at the enemy. At the order, they will all ride forward at the same time.

Getting it right

For a cavalry charge to be really effective, you had to have the right conditions. Open spaces and reasonably flat ground worked best, as uneven ground slowed down the horses. A gentle slope down towards the enemy was even better, as it speeded up the knights' charge. It was vital that knights all charged together. If a few knights charged before they received the order, the whole battle could be lost.

38

The Battle of Crécy

Fighting in a way that best suited the terrain won and lost battles. In the Battle of Crécy, fought in France in 1346 between the English and French, the battleground was uneven and riddled with holes deliberately dug by the English. The English knights, led by King Edward III and his son, the Black Prince, dismounted to fight on foot, and made full use of their longbowmen. But the French knights, led by King Philip VI, charged in their usual way. In the end, this lost them the battle. Here you can see what happened.

Key:
- French crossbowmen
- French knights
- English longbowmen
- English knights
- Advance
- Retreat

1

At the start of the battle, Edward arranged his army in three groups at the top of the hill.

Philip's knights outnumbered the English, but were less organized. They were positioned at the bottom of the hill.

2

Philip commanded his crossbowmen to advance and fire. While they were reloading their bows, the English longbowmen fired on them, killing hundreds.

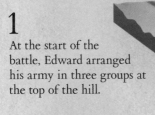

The French bowmen begin to retreat.

3

Ignoring orders, French knights charged at the English, trampling down their own bowmen. Struggling over the difficult terrain and obstacles, many were killed by the relentless rain of English arrows.

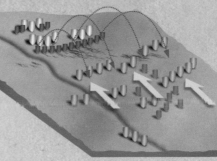

4

The French knights kept on attacking, but the English knights stood their ground, refusing to break ranks: they simply watched while their longbowmen slaughtered the French.

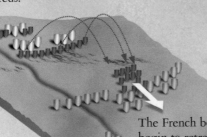

5

The French charged on the Black Prince, but were defeated after fierce fighting.

The French knights retreat.

Life on campaign

All medieval battles were fierce and bloody, but the perils of war weren't just limited to being killed in action. Life on campaign was harsh too. Your life could be cut short at any time by disease or even starvation. And if you survived the battle, but were on the losing side, imprisonment was the very best you could hope for.

Long-distance travel

When wars took place hundreds of miles away, the journey must have seemed like half the battle. Transportation was always a problem. All the equipment, and as much food as you could carry, had to be transported to the war zone - in wagons, by horses or, if you were really unlucky, on your back. But there was a limit to how much you could carry. So after a while food supplies were bound to run out. On long campaigns, armies had to rely on finding food as they moved through the countryside. This usually meant stealing from farms and looting villages.

If you were very lucky, you might have a wagon to help carry your equipment.

Most ordinary soldiers had to carry what they needed. If they had to get to a battle quickly, they could be exhausted before it even began.

The knights in this medieval painting are sailing across the Irish Sea to England. Although the journey isn't very far, the Irish Sea was notoriously rough and dangerous.

All at sea

When a war was being fought overseas, knights and other soldiers sometimes had to be packed onto ships to travel to the battlefield. Sea voyages – especially long ones – could be fatal. Disease was commonplace, and living in close quarters meant that infections spread quickly. Fresh food soon ran out and without a good diet soldiers became ill. On top of this, there was the risk of running into pirates, and bad storms could wreck ships in minutes. Many soldiers just never made it.

For a link to a website where you can pretend to be a squire and prepare a knight for battle, go to www.usborne-quicklinks.com

Knights rode on their spare horses, saving their destriers for the fight itself. Their armor was carried by packhorses.

No mercy

Knights had set rules about how to behave on the battlefield. Waving a white flag signaled defeat and meant everyone was supposed to stop fighting. You were not supposed to kill knights on the losing side; they were usually held for ransom instead. This meant being kept prisoner until their friends or relatives paid a fee for their release. But knights were not obliged to treat simple foot soldiers with such consideration. These poor soldiers were often simply slaughtered on the spot.

The French knight in this medieval painting is being taken prisoner. It's likely that he was well treated by his captors, until a fee was paid for his release.

Under siege

A lot of medieval warfare involved surrounding towns and castles, and trying to capture them. This was called siege warfare. If you managed to take over a town or castle, you won more than a new base to fight from. You got control of the surrounding land too.

Siege strategies

If you were attacking a castle, you could start by setting up camp outside and trying to starve it into surrender, by stopping supplies from getting through. But there was a danger that you and your army would run out of food too, and living conditions in the camps were usually so unhygienic that there were frequent outbreaks of deadly diseases. Rather than risk all this, most armies tried to capture a castle as quickly as possible. The most effective way was to destroy parts of it and get inside. Soldiers used a number of tactics to do this, many involving huge weapons called siege engines.

This is a battering ram. Inside, there's a tree trunk that's swung back and forth against walls, doors and gates, to bash them down.

The soldiers on the left are using a missile-throwing device called a *trebuchet*.

These soldiers are digging a tunnel under the castle walls to make them collapse. The fence protects the soldiers and hides what they are doing.

Down and under

Siege engines weren't the only way to bring down castle walls. You could dig under (undermine) them to make them collapse. Soldiers dug a tunnel, then propped it up with wooden beams. Then they stuffed it with fat-soaked sticks and set them alight. The props burned down, making the tunnel collapse, so the castle wall above fell down too.

The battering ram and the siege tower are covered with soaking-wet animal skins, to try to protect them from fire.

Messy missiles

Missile-throwing siege engines, such as *trebuchets*, were used to fling heavy stones at the fortress. Sometimes dead animals – or even the heads of enemy soldiers – were catapulted over. The idea was to spread disease and give the enemy a shock!

Scaling ladders, used to climb walls, are cheaper than siege towers. But they can be pushed away from the wall, sending attacking soldiers plummeting to their deaths.

Siege towers, or *belfries*, allow soldiers to climb to the top of the walls under cover. Then they can drop a drawbridge across and clamber onto the walls.

43

On the defense

When a castle or fortress was under attack, the people inside had plenty of ways of fending off their attackers. A good castle builder always tried to give his fortress a fighting chance by making it hard to attack. He might build it in a hard-to-reach place, on a hilltop, or dig a water-filled ditch, called a *moat*, around it. Clever defense tactics were also crucial for surviving a siege.

Gaps in the walls (called crenels) give defending archers room to fire arrows.

Arrow loop

Arrow loops

Defending soldiers had the advantage of being able to hurl missiles at the enemy from behind the relative safety of the walls. Archers fired arrows out of slits, called *arrow loops*, which were wider on the inside than on the outside. It was easy to fire arrows out, but it was much harder to shoot them in.

A battering ram

Missiles dropped from above bounce off the sloping base of the walls at unpredictable angles, scattering attackers.

These curved walls are far harder to break down than straight ones.

44

Hurling missiles

In the early days of castles, wooden platforms were built on top of the walls. They stuck out over the walls and had holes in the floor. The idea was to give defenders a sheltered place from which to drop missiles down onto their enemies. By the 14th century, these had started to become permanent fixtures made of stone, called *machicolations*.

Hot sand and rocks are thrown through holes in stone platforms, known as machicolations.

Counterattack

The only way to prevent undermining was to countermine – to dig another tunnel to try to meet up with the enemy's tunnel. Then, the two sides fought it out underground until one side lost. But how could the defenders tell when the castle was being undermined in the first place? One method was to place bowls of water on the ground. Ripples in the water, caused by vibrations in the ground, were a telltale sign of work going on down below.

For a link to a website where you can build a trebuchet online and try to destroy a castle, go to **www.usborne-quicklinks.com**

Wooden platforms could be built quickly for extra protection when a castle was under threat of siege.

These soldiers are digging a tunnel to intercept the attackers' tunnel.

Last resorts

Often, all these tactics enabled defenders to hold out until help arrived. But if it didn't look as if anyone was going to turn up in time, there were only two alternatives: hang on until the castle crumbled and expect no mercy from the enemy, or surrender. Surrendering was definitely safer. You might lose the castle, but you could often persuade your enemies to spare your lives – provided they stuck to their side of the bargain.

Heraldry and heralds

This knight is dressed for a tournament. His coat of arms helps the audience to recognize him.

Full armor was essential for keeping knights safe, but it also made it very difficult to tell who was who in the thick of battle. This could be especially nasty if someone on your own side mistook you for the enemy. So, from the early 12th century, knights began to use distinctive, brightly-painted patterns and symbols on their shields to identify each other. These came to be known as coats of arms. The study of coats of arms is called heraldry.

Arms all over

At first, the coat of arms was painted on a knight's shield. But shields were often damaged or lost in battle, so knights began to add it to other parts of their armor too. From the end of the 13th century, to make things even easier, they also wore their coats of arms on cloth tunics on top of their armor. By the 14th century, their helmets even had crests to match.

Seal of approval

Coats of arms spread quickly from the battlefield into everyday life. Soon, all kinds of things, from furniture to entire buildings, were decorated with them. Knights had seals with their arms on them, and used them to stamp official documents.

But a coat of arms was always a privilege and it could be taken away if a knight misbehaved. If a knight was found guilty of betraying his lord or king, he could have his coat of arms confiscated and his shield hung upside down, as a public sign of his disgrace.

Rules and regulations

Over time, coats of arms became increasingly complicated, as more and more noble families wanted to have them. Rules developed to control how colors, patterns and designs could be combined. This helped avoid confusion by making sure each family had its own distinctive arms. But it became more and more difficult to remember all of them. So, eventually, men called heralds were appointed to take charge.

These arms are from a document known as a roll of arms. Heralds painted arms on the roll to keep a record of them.

For a link to a website where you can play a heraldry game and learn more about coats of arms, go to www.usborne-quicklinks.com

If a knight was very badly injured in battle, the only way to identify him was to ask a herald to examine his coat of arms.

Heralds in charge

At first, a herald's job was simply to identify contestants at tournaments, but knights soon realized how useful they could be on the battlefield too. After all, a herald was the best person to recognize all the other knights and, more importantly, the enemy. Soon, every knight wanted to have his own herald on call. In peacetime, they had their uses too, organizing ceremonies, pageants and even weddings and funerals for their employers.

Eventually, heralds were put in charge of the whole system of heraldry, keeping official records of heraldic designs and inventing coats of arms for new knights. In some countries, a college of arms was set up, where records were kept and young men could train to be heralds. Trainee heralds were known as *pursuivants*.

Coats of arms

Coats of arms come in many colors, with all sorts of different pictures and patterns on them. Heralds used special words to describe them, which come from medieval French and are still used today. Here you can read about some of the terms used, and some of the rules for how to create new coats of arms.

For a link to a website where you can find out how to design your own coat of arms, go to **www.usborne-quicklinks.com**

The basic arms

Coats of arms are usually shield-shaped, because they were originally painted on shields. They are divided into different parts - the most basic parts are known as the *field*, *ordinaries* and *charges*.

Describing a coat of arms is called *blazoning*, and in heraldry it's always done in a particular order. You start by describing the field – what color it is, for example - then the ordinary, then the way the field is divided and, finally, the charges.

Dexter means right.*

Chief means the top.

Sinister means left.*

The *charge* is a design above the *field* or *ordinaries*. It can be a pattern or picture.

Ordinaries are bands of color. They can be different shapes. This ordinary is called a *fess*.

Fess means middle.

The *field* is the arms' background.

Base means bottom.

Colors

There were originally four basic colors in heraldry - black, red, green and blue - as well as metallic colors silver and gold. Patterns were also used to represent furry textures, such as *ermine* (stoat) and *vair* (squirrel).

As more and more people wanted coats of arms, more colors and furs were added to the basic list. Below you can see some of the different colors, metals and furs, with their heraldic names in italics.

Vert
(green)

Sable
(black)

Gules
(red)

Azure
(blue)

Purpure
(purple)

Or
(gold)

Argent
(silver)

Ermine
(stoat)

Vair
(squirrel)

* From the knight's point of view when he's holding the shield.

48

Joining and dividing

Coats of arms could be divided up so you could combine two or more different arms on the same shield. This was done when two families were joined together by a marriage. There were five ways of dividing up a field:

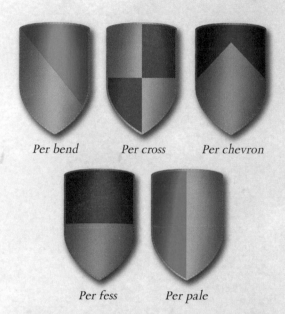

Per bend   Per cross   Per chevron

Per fess   Per pale

In a shield divided *per pale*, the husband's coat of arms would be placed on the right-hand side of the shield (*dexter*) and the wife's family's arms on the left (*sinister*). This is known as *impaling*.

Later, even more divisions were introduced. Here are some of them.

Paly   Barry   Bendy   Barry wavy

Checky   Paly wavy   Lozengy   Gyronny

Meanings and symbols

Sometimes, the patterns and pictures on coats of arms had special meanings. For example, a bee sometimes stood for efficiency and a boar for bravery or protection. Knights often used symbols with meanings which they thought reflected their personality, their family history or their name. But it was the senior heralds who ultimately decided which symbols you could have.

Here are some of the meanings of different charges. They could vary from one place or time to another.

Swords: justice   Snake: healing   Bear: strength or cunning   Lion: bravery

Arms for all the family

A whole family shared the same basic coat of arms. But different individuals added their own marks, known as marks of cadency, to create their own unique arms. Only the head of the family could use the family coat of arms without these extra marks. Women didn't have their own coats of arms. An unmarried woman used her father's arms on a diamond shape, rather than a shield shape.

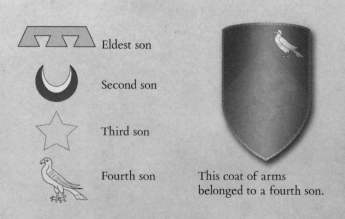

Eldest son

Second son

Third son

Fourth son

This coat of arms belonged to a fourth son.

This painting from a medieval manuscript shows King Louis IX of France setting off on the Seventh Crusade in 1248.

Crusaders

Crusaders were knights who were sent by the Church to fight in religious wars against its enemies. Eight major crusades were fought in the Middle East, against Muslims, each side fighting for control of an area people called the Holy Land. The Holy Land included the city of Jerusalem, and it was important to the Church because Jesus had lived and died there. For centuries, Christians had gone on journeys, called pilgrimages, to pray there.

How it started

In around 1040, the Seljuk Turks, a new group of Muslim rulers, took power in the Holy Land. They were hostile to Christians and so Christians were no longer welcome there. European rulers and churchmen began to worry that the Seljuks would try to expand their territory into Europe too. In 1095, the Pope called on Christian knights all across Europe to go on a crusade to free Jerusalem from the Turks.

Crusader craze

The Pope only intended knights to go to the Holy Land, but ordinary people soon caught the crusading craze. In the spring of 1096, thousands of men and women, and even children, set out for the Holy Land in an unruly mob. It became known as the 'People's Crusade.' Many died along the way from disease, or were killed in skirmishes by Turkish troops. Others caused chaos, looting and attacking wherever they went. Few, if any of them, ever reached the Holy Land.

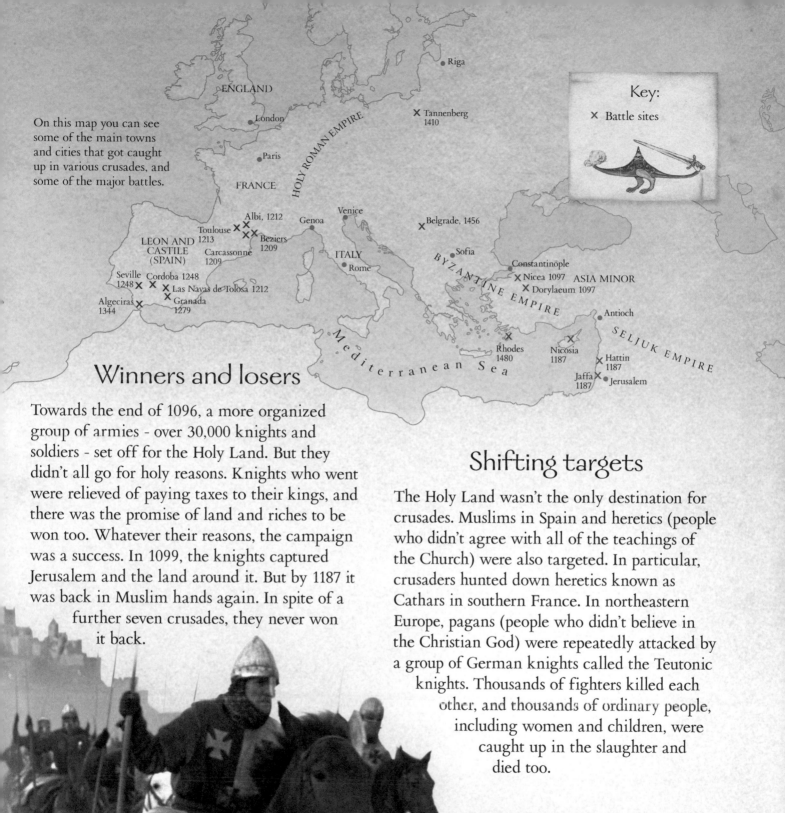

On this map you can see some of the main towns and cities that got caught up in various crusades, and some of the major battles.

Key:
× Battle sites

Riga

ENGLAND

London

HOLY ROMAN EMPIRE

× Tannenberg 1410

Paris

FRANCE

Albi, 1212

Toulouse 1213 ×

Genoa

Venice

× Belgrade, 1456

× ×

LEON AND CASTILE (SPAIN)

× Beziers 1209

Carcassonne 1209

ITALY

Rome

Sofia

BYZANTINE EMPIRE

Constantinople

× Nicea 1097   ASIA MINOR

× Dorylaeum 1097

Seville 1248 ×

Cordoba 1248

× × Las Navas de Tolosa 1212

Antioch

Algeciras 1344 ×

× Granada 1279

Mediterranean Sea

Rhodes 1480 ×

Nicosia 1187 ×

SELJUK EMPIRE

× Hattin 1187

Jaffa × 1187

Jerusalem

Winners and losers

Towards the end of 1096, a more organized group of armies - over 30,000 knights and soldiers - set off for the Holy Land. But they didn't all go for holy reasons. Knights who went were relieved of paying taxes to their kings, and there was the promise of land and riches to be won too. Whatever their reasons, the campaign was a success. In 1099, the knights captured Jerusalem and the land around it. But by 1187 it was back in Muslim hands again. In spite of a further seven crusades, they never won it back.

Shifting targets

The Holy Land wasn't the only destination for crusades. Muslims in Spain and heretics (people who didn't agree with all of the teachings of the Church) were also targeted. In particular, crusaders hunted down heretics known as Cathars in southern France. In northeastern Europe, pagans (people who didn't believe in the Christian God) were repeatedly attacked by a group of German knights called the Teutonic knights. Thousands of fighters killed each other, and thousands of ordinary people, including women and children, were caught up in the slaughter and died too.

In this scene from the movie *Kingdom of Heaven*, directed by Ridley Scott, knights are riding into battle during the Third Crusade (1189-1193).

For a link to a website where you can find a timeline of the First Crusade and play some games, go to www.usborne-quicklinks.com

51

Templars and Hospitallers

Early on in the crusades, permanent forces of knights were set up in the Holy Land to protect territory and to guide people on their way to holy sites. Two of these groups were particularly important: the Order of the Hospital of St. John (known as the Hospitallers) and the Order of the Temple (known as the Templars). These knights took religious vows, but were soldiers too, and they were just as ruthless in battle as any other crusading knight.

The Templars eventually came to a sticky end. Many were even burned to death, like the ones in this medieval painting.

The rise ...

The Templars and the Hospitallers gradually became very wealthy and powerful, as kings and lords donated money and land to them. This meant that they were able to build impressive fortresses, and they created the biggest fleets of ships in Europe. As members of religious orders, they only had to obey the Pope, rather than any king. This gave them a lot more power than ordinary knights.

... and fall

But their great wealth meant that they soon attracted the envy of kings and nobles. Matters came to a head in 1310, when King Philip IV of France (who just happened to owe them money) accused the Templars of worshipping devils and being heretics. The Church had thousands of them tortured until they confessed. After this, the Templars were forced to break up and their possessions were seized. But, according to legend, most of their treasure was whisked away before anyone else could get their hands on it.

Templars and Hospitallers wore particular colors so they stood out from ordinary knights. This knight is wearing a Templar's costume: a white tunic with a red cross on it.

A lucky escape

Although the Hospitallers were just as wealthy and powerful, they managed to escape the same fate. This could have been because they did charitable work and so had more popular support. In 1187, Jerusalem was captured by Muslim forces and the Hospitallers moved to Rhodes. When Rhodes was also taken by Muslims in 1522, they moved to Malta. The Hospitallers disbanded in the 1700s, but reappeared in the 19th century as the Order of St. John, which still exists today. Nowadays it's a charity doing medical work, rather than fighting.

Castle strongholds

Many crusader castles in the Holy Land are still standing today. These castles, often built on the sites of captured Muslim castles, were extremely strong. Water supplies were often a problem in the hot climate, especially during sieges, so some had large stone-lined water tanks sunk in the ground beneath them. The castle of Krac des Chevaliers, in Syria, had an underground chamber big enough to store food for a five-year siege.

Krac des Chevaliers was built by the Hospitallers between 1142 and 1271. About 4,000 knights were once based there.

Other religious knights

The Teutonic knights were a group of German knights, founded during the Third Crusade. From the 13th century, they campaigned in eastern Europe, conquering huge tracts of land from pagan peoples who lived there. Spanish military orders, such as the Knights of Calatrava and the Knights of St. James of Compostela, were formed in the 12th century. They went on crusades to regain parts of Spain that had been conquered by Muslims.

For a link to a website where you can find a timeline, and lots of facts about crusader castles in the Middle East, go to
www.usborne-quicklinks.com

Fighting back

European crusaders in the Holy Land faced a formidable foe. The Muslim armies were well equipped and cleverly commanded, and their fighters came from different parts of Asia and the Middle East. Many were accomplished soldiers and each had their own specialist ways of fighting and using weapons.

This Turcoman fighter is wielding a sword, but the Turcomans were also highly skilled archers.

Expert archers

Many of the Muslim armies defending the Holy Land contained Turcoman tribesmen from Central Asia. They were famous for their skills as archers, both on foot and on horseback. Troops known as Ghulams fought alongside the Turcomans. They were slaves and prisoners of war who served as professional full-time soldiers. Like the Turcomans, they were highly skilled archers. They could shoot five arrows every two and a half seconds. But they also used spears, swords and maces.

For a link to a website where you can read more about Saladin, go to **www.usborne-quicklinks.com**

Ghulams formed the bulk of the Seljuk army. This one is protected by chain mail and scale mail - tiny pieces of overlapping metal that look like fish scales.

Flaming grenades

Arab and Kurdish soldiers wore fabric-covered chain mail tunics and sturdy helmets. They fought with swords and spears and carried large, round shields. Some rode on horseback, but many others fought on foot - including archers and soldiers armed with long-reach weapons, such as spears and pikes.

Foot soldiers also used a type of grenade. It contained a substance called naphtha, which went up in flames very easily. It was a particularly nasty weapon. It burned with an intense heat, was very hard to put out, and stuck to anything it came into contact with, including skin.

This medieval English picture shows a Muslim and a crusader fighting. The Muslim has been made to look like a devil.

Saladin

The most famous Muslim leader in the crusades was Salah al Din Yusuf ibn Ayyub, known in Europe as Saladin. He led the opposition to the crusaders from around 1169 until his death in 1193. During this time, he captured around 50 crusader castles and took control of the city of Jerusalem and most of the lands around it. Although he was an enemy, Saladin was respected throughout Europe as an accomplished and noble fighter, and a deeply religious man.

This 15th century painting shows the Battle of Hattin, fought between Saladin's men and crusading knights. Only 3,000 crusaders out of an 80,000-strong army escaped from the pass.

Locking horns

Saladin's most famous victory was in a mountain pass known as the Horns of Hattin. Here, in 1187, his troops trapped the army of Guy of Lusignan, a French knight who had been crowned King of Jerusalem by the crusaders. After a desperate fight, Guy and most of his troops were forced to surrender. News of the disaster prompted a third crusade, although it took two years for it to get under way.

Eastern knights

In the Middle Ages, soldiers on horseback were by no means unique to Europe and the Middle East. Elite mounted warriors existed in parts of Asia too, and their weapons, equipment and tactics were sometimes surprisingly similar.

Samurai warriors

From the 12th to the 19th centuries, Japan was under the control of a powerful group of soldiers, known as *samurai*. Like knights, they fought on horseback, and wore metal helmets and armor made from leather or metal plates to protect them in battle. Samurai believed one-to-one combat was the most honorable way of fighting. Unlike knights, some were also excellent archers.

The way of the warrior

Samurai lived by a very strict code of conduct, known as *bushido*, or 'the way of the warrior,' which affected every part of their lives. Loyalty and honor were especially important. If a samurai failed to keep to the code, he might be expected to commit suicide.

Samurai were organized in strict ranks - from the ruler, called the *shogun*, to the *daiymos*, the warrior warlords, down to the lowest-ranking fighter. The way a samurai was supposed to behave depended on his rank. Stepping outside these boundaries could end in death.

This 17th century samurai armor from Japan is made from metal, covered with red lacquer.

A samurai sword

Horsemen of the plains

The Mongols, from the plains of central Asia, were fierce and formidable horseback-riding warriors, famous for moving at incredible speed in all weathers. Led by their ferocious ruler, Genghis Khan, in the 13th century, they swept down into Russia and invaded central Europe. The Mongols were immensely successful fighters and soon gained a reputation for cunning and ruthlessness, using surprise tactics to confuse their enemy.

In this scene from the BBC programme *Genghis Khan*, Mongol soldiers gallop into battle. The Mongols fought with a whole range of weaponry: bows and arrows, swords and lances, and even primitive grenades.

A formidable foe

One of the keys to the Mongols' success was their highly organized, disciplined and well-trained armies. They planned all their campaigns rigorously: gathering intelligence about the enemy in advance, deciding exactly how the war was to be waged, and setting a strict timetable for each campaign. In battle, orders were efficiently relayed from one part of the army to another by shouts, drumbeats and flag signals. Another of the Mongols' strengths was that they were very adaptable. They were happy to recruit new soldiers from conquered peoples, and to copy and use any new weapons and tactics they came across.

This knight is about to
fight in a competition
called a joust.

Knights at peace

Even when knights weren't at war, they still spent a
lot of time training and practicing their fighting
skills. Many had to help protect their overlord's castle
for a fixed number of days each year. But life wasn't
all about fighting. When knights weren't looking
after the day-to-day running of their estates, there
were plenty of other more relaxing things to do.

Training to be a knight

The sons of knights were expected to become knights too, unless they became priests or monks instead. Very young trainee knights, known as pages, were usually sent away to another knight's castle to learn the tricks of the trade. There, they spent the first few years learning basic fighting skills and how to behave in society.

Pages have to attend knights at the table, to learn good manners.

Pages wrestle to increase their strength and fitness, as well as to improve their fighting skills.

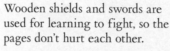
Wooden shields and swords are used for learning to fight, so the pages don't hurt each other.

This page is sitting on a wooden horse, so he can practice couching a lance while riding.

The next step

When a page had become skilled enough, the next step was to become a squire. Squires often lived and trained together in small groups. They learned to hunt, had music and dancing lessons, and were taught how to treat women properly. They continued to practice their sword fighting and riding skills too, and learned how to charge with a lance. Riding at targets, known as *quintains*, helped a squire to become more accurate with a lance, and to become a good rider.

The squire aims his lance at the target and rides towards it.

If he hits it squarely, a weight swings around and the squire has to duck.

A squire's work

A squire worked as an apprentice to a knight, and was supposed to watch and learn from the knight's behavior. His duties included helping the knight prepare for battles and tournaments, and looking after and carrying his equipment. A squire usually stayed at the edge of the action, holding extra weapons and horses in case the knight lost his. He would help the knight if he was wounded. After the battle, he helped him to disarm and took care of his horses.

This squire is helping his knight put his armor on in preparation for battle.

This knight has been wounded and needs his squire's help to leave the battlefield.

After the battle, it's the squire's duty to make sure that someone cleans and polishes the knight's armor and weapons.

The final step

When a squire was considered to be skilled enough at fighting, it was time for him to become a fully-fledged knight. This happened in a knighting ceremony. The squire was 'knighted' by a king, or a senior knight. During the ceremony, the new knight was supposed to receive his spurs (spikes worn on the heels to make a horse move faster) and a sword, as symbols of his new status. In practice, a squire was often knighted on campaign - or even during a battle - whenever new knights were needed urgently. When a squire had been knighted, he was called 'Sir.'

When a squire was 'knighted,' he was tapped on the shoulders. This is known as dubbing. It was the symbol of becoming a knight.

A squire for life

Not all squires became knights. Many simply couldn't afford all the armor and horses a knight needed. Being a squire was a perfectly respectable job. A highly-trained squire could have a very successful career in the army without ever being knighted, and well-educated squires could easily find work in castles and courts all over Europe.

For a link to a website where you can find out about becoming a knight and dress a knight in armor, go to **www.usborne-quicklinks.com**

Feasting and fun

Really well-off knights had their own castle - and sometimes even several castles - as well as houses, farms and land. But almost all knights had some land to return to in times of peace. When they were at home, they liked to relax and enjoy themselves, and there was plenty of opportunity for feasting and fun.

Food and drink

Knights often held feasts and a good host always provided generous amounts of food for his guests. Medieval feasts were often elaborate, with huge amounts of food. For extra special occasions, exotic birds, such as peacock, crane and even vulture, were served, as well as the more usual beef and pork. There were strict rules about who could eat what - and only the most important guests were served the whole menu.

A banquet wasn't complete without a whole host of entertainers: acrobats, jugglers, minstrels (musicians), troubadours (poets) and jesters (comedians and storytellers). Sometimes, short plays, known as *interludes*, were staged in between courses. They often had religious or moral themes, which were supposed to educate the guests, as well as amuse them.

Games and pastimes

Knights and their households enjoyed playing card games and games with dice. Board games, such as chess, and a game called *merrills* - a complicated version of tic-tac-toe - were also popular. Although most ordinary people couldn't read, many knights enjoyed reading stories, as well as consulting handbooks on hunting and on knightly codes of honor.

The less important you are, the further away you sit from the knight and his guests.

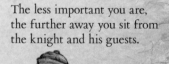

The minstrel on the left is playing a harp, while the minstrel on the right is tuning a viol (a type of medieval violin).

Running the manor

Life in a castle wasn't all fun and games. Its day-to-day running could be hard work. The knight had to make sure rent was being collected, that enough supplies for the castle were ordered in, and that his farms were being managed properly. There were always disputes to be settled among the tenants too.

This jester is trying to make his lord laugh.

Important guests sit with the knight at a raised table.

These diners are eating food off slabs of bread, called *trenchers*. The trenchers will be given to the poor to eat after the meal.

For a link to a website where you can find some interesting medieval recipes, go to **www.usborne-quicklinks.com**

Hunting and hawking

Knights enjoyed hunting in their spare time, but it wasn't just about having fun. It helped them keep in practice with their riding and weaponry skills, as well as providing meat and furs. Knights hunted a wide variety of animals, including deer, boars, wolves and bears - that were all common in Europe in the Middle Ages.

Ladies and knights ride on horses during the hunt. Servants have to try to keep up on foot.

When they catch sight of the deer, the hunters will try to slow it down using spears. A servant is on stand-by with extra spears.

The thrill of the chase

Deer, or stag, hunting was considered the noblest sport of all. But the hunt started long before the nobles were even awake. Huntsmen scoured the woods and fields for fresh deer tracks. When they found them, the hunting dogs were brought out. As soon as the dogs caught the deer's scent, the nobles joined the hunting party, and they all set off in swift pursuit. When they caught up with the deer, a huntsman killed it with a long knife.

Happy hunting

Nobles hunted in areas set aside just for them. As no one else was allowed to hunt there, it meant that there were always plenty of animals around. There were strict rules about what ordinary people could hunt and eat. Peasants received terrible punishments if they dared to poach animals reserved for the nobles. They could even be killed for it.

The huntsmen carry horns, to help them find each other if they are separated in the forest, and to encourage the dogs.

Hunting with birds

Noblemen and women also hunted with tamed birds of prey, such as kestrels and falcons. This was known as hawking, or falconry. These birds were trained from a young age, so that they became tame and used to people. They learned to sit on the hand of their master or mistress, and fly off to kill animals. Birds could be trained to catch small animals on the ground, such as rabbits, or other, smaller birds in the air.

This man is wearing thick leather gloves to protect his hands from the bird's talons.

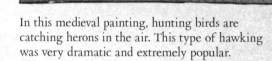

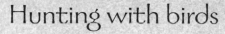

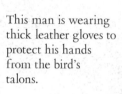

In this medieval painting, hunting birds are catching herons in the air. This type of hawking was very dramatic and extremely popular.

An expensive hobby

Keeping hunting birds reflected your status in society. Kings hunted with birds called gyrfalcons, barons hunted with buzzards, and ordinary knights hunted with smaller birds called sacrets. Hunting birds were expensive to buy, train and feed, and were kept in special buildings called *mews*. Nobles often spent a fortune on their birds, and some even bought extravagant accessories for them, such as jewel-covered hoods.

For a link to a website where you can find illuminated manuscripts showing hawking and other scenes from medieval life, go to **www.usborne-quicklinks.com**

Tournaments

Tournaments were mock battles between groups or pairs of mounted knights, which gave them a chance to show off their fighting skills. Tournaments started off as training exercises, but soon caught on as a popular sport. By the 12th century, they were all the rage throughout western Europe.

Free-for-all

The earliest tournaments, known as mêlées, were just huge free-for-alls, with lots of mounted knights fighting each other out in the countryside. Each knight tried to defeat and capture another knight. Whoever succeeded could seize his opponent's horse and armor and force him to pay for their return. Knights weren't supposed to kill each other, but many did die - either by accident, or because their opponents just got carried away.

Jousting

From the end of the 12th century, new types of competitions were introduced. In one contest, known as a pas d'armes, a single knight challenged all comers to defeat him in a specific task, such as capturing a bridge he was defending. In another contest, called a joust, pairs of knights rode towards each other and fought on horseback. Each tried to hit the other, using a lance, to score points. Enclosed areas, called lists, were set aside for mêlées and jousts, to try to cut down on serious injuries.

In this joust, a knight scores points for hitting his opponent's shield.

The impact of this knight's lance has broken the lance of his opponent (on the right).

The knight on the right wins this joust by knocking his opponent off his horse.

Blunt instruments

Despite new competitions and more orderly contests, knights continued to die in tournaments throughout the Middle Ages. To try to take away some of the danger, contestants used specially made blunt weapons made of wood or whalebone. Some jousting lances had crown-shaped tips, called coronels. This spread the impact of the blow, making it less likely to pierce armor. When a knight hit his opponent, the lance either shattered, or knocked the other knight off his horse.

Coronel —

Party tricks

By the 1500s, tournaments had become so safe that the contests alone weren't enough to satisfy the watching crowds. So extra gimmicks were introduced to keep them amused. In Germany, knights sometimes wore trick breastplates and carried trick shields, which burst apart in a spectacular explosion when an opponent struck them in the right place.

A direct hit with a lance triggers a spring-loaded mechanism, hidden in the knight's shield, making it explode dramatically.

Fight to the death

However many safety measures were taken, tournaments could still be dangerous, and accidents continued to happen – sometimes fatal ones. This was inevitable when men rode into each other at great speed, wielding pointed implements. But if you were a particularly unscrupulous knight, you could also use a tournament as a good opportunity to get rid of your rival, by disguising murder as an accident.

This medieval painting shows a knight who has been fatally wounded during a tournament.

This medieval painting
shows a brave knight
killing a dragon.

Knights and chivalry

Medieval knights were brave, loyal and merciful. They protected the weak and fought fairly against their enemies. Or, at least, that was the theory. The code of behavior that knights were supposed to live by was known as chivalry. Although knights often didn't behave in a chivalrous way, chivalry was still a very important part of being a knight. It inspired poems and songs – and perhaps even changed the way knights thought about women.

A perfect knight

Lots of handbooks were written in the Middle Ages about how knights ought to behave. They laid out exactly what it meant to be a knight and what duties were expected of them. Different authors had different ideas about what a knight should be. But loyalty, honor and courtesy were always high on the list, followed by prowess, hardiness, faith and humility.

Loyalty and honor

Loyalty and honor were at the very heart of chivalry. All knights swore oaths of loyalty to their overlord and their king. Nothing could justify disloyalty - even if being loyal resulted in death. Being a 'man of honor' meant being honest, never breaking a promise and never doing anything to disgrace your family name. So it was a matter of honor that a knight always kept any promises of loyalty he had made.

The knight in this medieval painting is kneeling before his lord as he pledges his loyalty to him. He offers up his sword, showing that he is willing to fight for him.

The lord in this painting behaves respectfully towards the lady, and keeps her amused.

Courtesy and largesse

Courtesy meant having good manners and knowing how to dress and behave in the right way. For a knight, it also meant being self-restrained in combat. For example, he should allow his enemy to get up again if he stumbled, and continue the fight, rather than slaughtering him on the spot. Knights were also expected to treat ladies, and more important knights, with respect, and to show *largesse*. This meant being as generous as you could afford to be, especially to less well-off knights.

Prowess and hardiness

Some aspects of chivalry had practical values, too. Knights not only had to fight skilfully, they were also supposed to take incredible risks and to continue fighting even when they were exhausted. *Prowess* was the knightly quality which involved skill and daring during combat. *Hardiness* required self-discipline and physical and mental courage. A hardy knight would always keep on going, however tough things got.

In this medieval painting, the legendary knight, Sir Lancelot, proves his prowess and hardiness by crossing a sword bridge, fighting a lion, and then battling with another knight.

For a link to a website where you can find out more about chivalry and medieval romances, go to **www.usborne-quicklinks.com**

Faith and humility

Faith in God was an essential part of being a knight. Knights' religious beliefs were supposed to support and guide them in everything they did, and give them the strength to survive difficult situations. Humility went hand in hand with faith. A humble knight believed that his achievements weren't due to his skill alone, but were gifts from God. So, the outcome of a battle was seen as God's will. Knights were encouraged not to be proud of their own abilities or to be over-confident in battle.

This knight shows his devotion to God by kneeling humbly as he vows to go and fight in a crusade.

Legends of chivalry

Real knights were never as chivalrous as the ones in medieval stories, but they still enjoyed reading tales of chivalry. Wealthy knights commissioned poets to write poems about legends of chivalry. Some of the stories were based on real-life adventures, but most of them described fantastical battles and impossible searches, known as quests.

Real-life heroes

The earliest stories of knights were stirring, and often bloodthirsty, tales about real, heroic warriors from the past. These stories were called *chansons de geste* (songs of deeds) and were performed by wandering minstrels who traveled from castle to castle. The hero of each story has many knightly virtues, but his most important quality is usually loyalty - to his lord, his fellow soldiers and his country. His loyalty is often put to the test when he is forced to choose between being disloyal and having to fight - especially when fighting means certain death.

The Song of Roland

The most famous *chanson* is the *Song of Roland*, which tells of the adventures of the nephew of Charlemagne, King of the Franks. At the most dramatic part of the story, Roland dies defending a mountain pass, rather than disobey his lord. Although Roland is fiercely loyal, he is too proud to call for help when he needs it.

In this medieval painting, Charlemagne finds the body of his dead nephew, Roland, after the Battle of Roncesvalles, in Spain, in 788.

New romantics

From the mid-12th century, a new type of poetry, known as a *roman*, became popular. The heroes of *romans* are usually solitary knights who ride off alone to look for adventure. The knight's goal is to prove himself to be the perfect knight. In many stories, this involves going on a quest or performing a difficult task. He may fail at first, but he usually learns from his mistakes and succeeds in the end.

The hero often falls in love, and is torn between his passion for his lady and his loyalty to his lord. For example, in the popular *roman, Tristan and Isolde,* Tristan's uncle, the King of Cornwall, is to marry Isolde. But Tristan and Isolde fall in love. Tragedy follows as they both try to stay loyal to the king, without being able to give up their love for one another.

The scene in this medieval painting is from *Tristan and Isolde.* While Tristan is escorting Isolde to Cornwall to marry his uncle, the king, the ill-fated couple falls in love.

Arthur and his knights

Some of the most famous *romans* were about King Arthur and his 'Knights of the Round Table.' The heroes in these tales have all sorts of exciting adventures, involving mythical beasts, damsels in distress, evil knights and magic. Some of Arthur's knights set out on the ultimate quest - the search for the Holy Grail. The Holy Grail was a mysterious holy object which some people thought was a cup which had once contained the blood of Jesus Christ. Only the purest knights, such as Sir Perceval and Sir Galahad, could even hope to attempt such a quest, never mind succeed in it. (You can find out more about these stories on pages 88-89.)

In this 14th century illumination, from the French *roman La Queste del Saint Graal*, Sir Galahad, Sir Perceval and Sir Bohors carry the Holy Grail to a safe place.

For a link to a website where you can find some more medieval *chansons* and *romans*, go to **www.usborne-quicklinks.com**

Knights and ladies

One of the most important aspects of chivalry was how to treat a lady. Knights were supposed to respect all women, but some poets also promoted the idea that a knight should devote himself to a particular lady who was completely out of reach. This hopeless love was meant to be pure and noble, and inspire the knight to do great things in her name. But where did this idea come from - and what happened in real life?

This decorative medieval parade shield shows a knight kneeling meekly before his lady.

Medieval knights were supposed to help ladies in need. This mid-15th century painting shows St. George killing a dragon and rescuing a princess.

Songs of love

In late 11th century France, poets known as *troubadours* began composing romantic love songs. The songs described the beauty and virtues of a lady. But they also told of the hopeless agonies a knight had to go through when he was in love with a woman he could not hope to win. Eventually, this developed into the idea of 'courtly love'. According to this, the ideal knight should act as the devoted servant of his lady, obeying all her orders and enduring harsh tests of his love.

For a link to a website where you can find out more about medieval ladies, go to **www.usborne-quicklinks.com**

Living the ideal

Most knights probably didn't take courtly love very seriously, except in a few extreme cases. An Austrian knight, Ulrich von Lichtenstein, rode around Europe wearing the figure of Venus, the goddess of love, on his helmet. Wherever he went, he challenged other knights to joust with him, in the hope that this would impress his lady.

Double standards

In fact, some knights treated noble ladies very badly. There are true stories of knights kidnapping and attacking them, and they showed even less respect for ordinary women. Medieval writers describe knights patrolling the streets of war-torn cities, completely ignoring the fact that 'common' women were being attacked all around them.

Knights and religion

In the Middle Ages, most people in Europe belonged to the
Roman Catholic Church. Religion was taken very seriously
and people believed that if they did anything wrong, they
might go to hell when they died. Knights were no exception.
Like all Christians, they tried to live virtuously, but it was
very hard to avoid killing people on the
battlefield - and killing people was
something the Church taught
was wrong, usually, anyway.

In this medieval painting, a
monk is giving a knight a
cross. This was a symbol to
show that it was acceptable
for him to go off to fight
in a crusade.

The Church's view

Early on, most priests condemned all killing,
but gradually this attitude changed. By the
11th century, fighting was officially allowed,
as long as it wasn't on holy days. Before big
battles, services were held to bless a knight's
banners and swords, and knights often hung
their shields in churches after a victory. But if
you killed someone in battle, you still had to
show you were sorry. This was called doing
penance. Penance usually meant praying for a
number of days, for each person you'd killed.

This could take up a lot of time, so wealthy
knights often paid monks to pray on their
behalf. When the First Crusade started in
1095, the Church positively encouraged
knights to kill - provided the victims were
enemies of the Church. Knights no longer had
to do penance, but many of them were still
afraid they might go to hell. So they left
money to pay for a priest to pray for them on a
regular basis, after they died, in the hope that
this would get them into heaven.

Crusader knights

The ultimate Christian knights were the crusaders, who swore an oath of allegiance to God, instead of swearing it to a king or lord. Crusaders wore the same kind of armor as other knights. But, instead of wearing a family coat of arms, they decorated their armor with a Christian cross. Some crusaders, such as the Templars and Hospitallers, even became monks, and pledged to fight for their faith.

This 12th century statue shows a French knight being greeted by his wife upon returning from crusades in the Holy Land.

For a link to a website where you can read more about the dramatic story of Thomas Becket's murder, go to **www.usborne-quicklinks.com**

Ungodly behavior

Not all knights lived up to the ideal of the perfect Christian knight. Many knights were more interested in their own fame and fortune than in the glory of God. Even crusaders became increasingly intent on keeping any riches they won to themselves. Medieval church sermons complained of knights who didn't live virtuously, who used foul language, and who didn't treat holy places with respect. One famous example of shocking knightly behavior took place in Canterbury Cathedral, England, in 1170, when the knights of King Henry II stabbed Archbishop Thomas Becket to death.

This image from a 15th century church altar shows Thomas Becket being murdered by knights while he kneels in prayer in Canterbury Cathedral.

The end of an era

By the 1500s, chivalry was on its way out and knights were no longer as important as they once had been. Armies were fighting in a different way. For some time, society had been changing too, as cities and towns replaced castles as centers of culture, trade and social life.

Walled towns like Carcassonne, in southwestern France, offered people everything castles could - and more.

New professional armies

By the end of the Middle Ages, many military leaders preferred to hire professional, well-trained, full-time soldiers, rather than relying on knights who only had to fight for a few months in the year. Soldiers in these new armies fought mainly on foot, using pikes, cannons and handguns. Heavily armored mounted knights were becoming a liability rather than an advantage. Plate armor couldn't stand up to cannon shot, and knights were in danger of being hooked clean off their horses by the enemy's pikes.

Early guns, like this one, were dangerous to use, as they sometimes exploded when fired. But, once guns were introduced, traditional medieval warfare began to go out of fashion.

Social changes

Meanwhile, life for the nobility was slowly changing too. They had far fewer peasants to farm their land and so they lost a lot of income. Going to war was becoming terribly expensive and some knights just couldn't afford to outfit themselves with armor and warhorses any more. So they stayed at home and looked after their estates instead. Some nobles didn't bother to be knighted at all; they just stayed as squires all their lives.

This medieval painting shows merchants buying and selling goods. Trade helped to make many of them wealthier than lords and kings, which made them very powerful.

The new knights

While knights were losing their position in society, merchants and traders were becoming more powerful and influential. Some became wealthy enough to lend money to the king, in exchange for a knighthood - even though they had no idea how to fight and would never need to. Many merchants married into noble families and acquired the title of knight that way. So eventually being a knight became a matter of wealth and status, and had nothing to do with riding on horseback in shining armor.

This knight is about to fight in single combat.

Knights fact file

Here you can find out about the lives of famous knights, read about some of the most dramatic battles in the Middle Ages, and discover more about the legend of King Arthur and the Knights of the Round Table. You will also find a glossary of knights, armor and weapons words.

Famous battles

Knights fact file

This picture is taken from the Bayeux tapestry, an enormous 70m (230ft) long tapestry. It was made to commemorate the Battle of Hastings, in 1066. In this section, the Normans are about to go into battle.

1066 The Battle of Hastings

The Battle of Hastings, fought in 1066 between the Normans and the English, was one of the most decisive battles in English history. In 1066, the English king, Edward the Confessor, died leaving no heir. There were three claimants for the throne: Harold Godwinson, a powerful English earl, Harald Hardraada, King of Norway, and Duke William of Normandy. The English chose Godwinson, which so enraged Hardraada that he invaded northern England. Godwinson defeated him, but had barely started celebrating when the news broke that William had invaded in the south. Immediately, Harold and his army set off on the long march back down south.

The two armies met near Hastings, on the south coast. Many of Harold's men had died in the battle in the north, and the rest were exhausted. But they were uphill from the enemy, and were able to bombard them with missiles. At first, all seemed lost for William, but he had one last trick up his sleeve. He ordered his men to pretend to run away. When some of Harold's men ran after them, William's men turned around and slaughtered them. After falling for this trick several times, Harold's defense was seriously weakened. William broke through the front line and won the battle. Harold, already wounded in the eye, was hacked to death.

1264 Battle of Lewes

The Battle of Lewes was fought in 1264 between rebellious English barons, led by Simon de Montfort, and the English king, Henry III. Things got off to a bad start for de Montfort when Henry's son, Prince Edward, broke through his defenses. But Edward then made a fatal mistake, by ordering his knights to chase some of de Montfort's men away from the battlefield. With the enemy knights out of the way, de Montfort made short work of the rest of Henry's army. After the battle, he had Henry shut away in the Tower of London. Simon de Montfort ruled England for a year, until he was killed in battle, in 1265, by Prince Edward's men.

This is a medieval painting of King Henry III.

82

In this medieval painting, soldiers are looting the city of Jerusalem after it has been taken by Christian crusaders.

1099 The siege of Jerusalem

The capture of Jerusalem, in 1099, was the most important victory in the First Crusade. In June 1099, Christian knights arrived at the Muslim controlled city of Jerusalem and began a siege that was to last for five weeks. Repeated attacks were made on the city walls, but it wasn't until the crusaders constructed siege engines that they were able to breach them.

Once inside the city, they set about massacring every man, woman and child they could find, Muslims and Jews, and even any Christian settlers who hadn't gotten out in time. It was said that the streets ran ankle-deep with their blood. After the battle, most of the crusaders went home, having done what they had set out to do - 'free' Jerusalem. The rest took control of the city. Few people in the city had survived the massacre, and any who had who were not Roman Catholics were promptly expelled from the city.

1212 Battle of Las Navas de Tolosa

The Battle of Las Navas de Tolosa, in southern Spain in 1212, ended in a spectacular victory for the Christian armies of Spain and Portugal over the Almohads - African Muslim Moors. For years, southern Spain and Portugal had been occupied by Muslims. But now they were beginning to expand their control northwards into land held by Christians, so the Pope called for a crusade against them. In 1212, Alfonso VIII of Castille joined up with Sancho VII of Navarre, Alfonso II of Portugal and Peter II of Aragon, and marched off to meet the Muslim army, led by Mohammed al-Nasir.

The two armies came face to face at Las Navas de Tolosa, northwest of Cordoba, on Friday 13th July. For a couple of days, there were only a few small, short-lived skirmishes, but on the Monday, the Christian forces made a full-on attack. After fierce fighting, Sancho and his men managed to break into the camp of al-Nasir, and broke up his line of defense. Al-Nasir escaped, but the rest of his soldiers were cut down by the Christians before they could flee. Over a 100,000 Muslim soldiers died in the battle. The defeat marked the beginning of the end for the Almohads in Spain and Portugal. Over the next 40 years, the Christians won victory after victory, reclaiming huge amounts of land and, by 1252, the Almohad empire was over.

For a link to a website where you can find out more about the Battle of Hastings, go to **www.usborne-quicklinks.com**

1240 Battle of the Neva

In 1240, an army led by Alexander, Prince of Novgorod, completely crushed the Swedish army at the Battle of Neva, in northern Russia. This halted the Swedish advance into Russia.

King Erik of Sweden had gathered together a huge army to invade northern Russia, and they hadn't expected much opposition. But, as soon as the Swedes landed on the banks of the river Neva, Alexander and his men set off to intercept them. They arrived at dawn, under the cover of thick fog, and at once attacked the Swedish camp. Completely taken by surprise, the Swedes were thrown into utter panic by the lightning speed of the attack. They tried to escape, but Alexander's men had cut their boats adrift from the riverbank. In honor of his victory, Alexander became known as Alexander 'Nevsky.'

This 16th century painting shows a scene from after the Battle of Agincourt: the English are killing French prisoners and stealing money and weapons from dead bodies.

1415 Battle of Agincourt

The Battle of Agincourt, in northern France, was one of the bloodiest battles of the Hundred Years War - a war fought by the English and French for control of land in France. By 1415, the war reached a new crisis point when Henry V, the new King of England, invaded France.

At the battle, the English were said to have been outnumbered by about four to one. It had been raining heavily, and the ground was covered in deep, thick mud. The French knights were the first to attack, but they couldn't charge because of the mud. When they reached the front line, many of their horses were injured on stakes the English had put in the ground. After a brief skirmish, they retreated. By the time the next wave of French soldiers attacked, the mud had been so churned up that many fell and were trampled by their own side, or suffocated. Others were killed by English longbowmen. After another onslaught by the English, the battle was won. The French had lost over 7,000 men in the space of just a few hours.

1485 Battle of Bosworth

The Battle of Bosworth, in 1485, marked the end of the Wars of the Roses, a 30-year struggle for power between rival families for the English throne. It was fought between Henry Tudor and Richard Duke of Gloucester, who had crowned himself Richard III. In 1485, the two armies met at Bosworth, near Leicester. From the start, the battle went badly for Richard. Rumors were spreading that he had murdered his nephews, and people believed them. He was now so unpopular that many of his men refused to fight. Some even swapped sides at the last minute. Faced with certain defeat, in a desperate attempt to win the day, Richard charged at Henry and his personal guard. Richard was quickly struck down and killed - and became the last British king to die on the battlefield. Henry was crowned king - and became the first king of the Tudor dynasty.

Henry Tudor, who is shown in this portrait, was crowned King Henry VII after the Battle of Bosworth.

This 16th century painting shows Charles the Bold, Duke of Burgundy, being killed during the Battle of Nancy, 1477.

1477 Battle of Nancy

The Battle of Nancy was a disastrous attempt by Charles the Bold, Duke of Burgundy, to capture Nancy, the capital of Lorraine, in France. Charles laid siege to Nancy in October 1466, and, by Christmas, the weather was appalling. Temperatures dropped, and blizzards raged. In one night alone, 400 Burgundian troops froze to death. But Charles was determined to hold out, even if it meant his men resorting to eating rats. Then, in January 1477, the Duke of Lorraine's reinforcements - Swiss mercenaries - arrived. The Burgundians were now vastly outnumbered. Charles and his army were soon surrounded and slaughtered. His mutilated body was found three days later, half-eaten by wolves.

For a link to a website where you can find out more about the Battle of Agincourt, and discover how important longbows were during the battle, go to **www.usborne-quicklinks.com**

Famous knights

Afew knights were so extraordinary that they became famous throughout Europe. Minstrels sang songs about their daring deeds, and chroniclers wrote of their bravery in battle. These remarkable men were the superstars of their day. Ordinary knights learned all they could about their heroes and tried to be just like them.

Rodrigo Díaz de Vivar (El Cid)
c. 1043–1099

Rodrigo Díaz de Vivar was famous for never losing a battle. Unusually for a Christian knight, he spent many years fighting for the Muslim Moors in Spain. The Moors called him El Cid, meaning 'the Lord,' but he was a hero for the Christians too. Born into a noble Spanish family, El Cid trained in the household of King Ferdinand II of Castile, in Spain, and became commander of the king's troops. But after Ferdinand's death he changed sides and fought for the Muslim ruler of the Spanish city of Saragossa. El Cid stayed with the Moors for ten years, before returning to serve a Christian king.

This 13th century picture of King Richard I of England was painted about 60 years after his death.

King Richard I (Richard the Lionheart)
1157–1199

Richard I of England was known as 'the Lionheart' because of his bravery and skill in battle. He was one of the leaders of the Third Crusade and captured the city of Acre from the Muslim leader Saladin. On his way back home, Richard was captured, and was handed over to the German emperor, who kept him prisoner until a large ransom was raised. Richard died after he was shot with a crossbow bolt during a siege and the wound became infected.

Godfrey de Bouillon
c. 1058–1100

Godfrey de Bouillon was a French knight who was given land in reward for his bravery in battle. In 1096, he joined the First Crusade, and sold most of his land to pay for the journey to the Holy Land. Godfrey was the hero of the siege of Jerusalem. After its capture, he was elected to rule the city. The crusaders offered him the title of king, but Godfrey was a pious man who lived simply, so he refused the title.

William Marshal
c. 1146–1219

William Marshal rose from fairly humble beginnings to become one of the most powerful men in England. His courage in the Hundred Years War earned him the job of military tutor to Prince Henry, son of King Henry II. Later, William served King Richard and King John, and acted as ambassador for England, negotiating deals with the French. William fought with the Templars in the crusades and was a major star on the tournament field. After Marshal's death, his servant wrote his biography, describing his master's noble deeds and adventures.

Bertrand du Guesclin
c. 1320–80

Bertrand du Guesclin was an outstanding French military commander. He fought many battles against the English during the Hundred Years War, and recaptured a huge amount of land. As well as being a courageous warrior, du Guesclin was an inspiring leader of men and a master of strategy who worked very hard to improve the quality of the French army.

This medieval painting shows du Guesclin being made Constable of France.

Edward the Black Prince
c. 1330–1376

Prince Edward was the eldest son of the English king, Edward III. He was knighted by his father at the age of 15, just before the Battle of Crécy. After that, he spent most of his time fighting the French in the Hundred Years War, although he also excelled in tournaments. Edward's most famous victory was the Battle of Poitiers, in 1356. Under his command, 7,000 English soldiers defeated a French force of 18,000, and also managed to capture the King of France. After his death, Edward became known as the Black Prince, probably because of the color of the armor he wore in battle.

Jean de Boucicaut
c. 1366–1421

Boucicaut was a French knight who began his career when he was just 16, fighting in the Hundred Years War against the English, and in the crusades. He was a stern commander with a passion for training and discipline. He was devoted to the knightly ideal of serving noble ladies. He formed the order of the White Lady of the Green Shield, whose members swore to protect the wives and daughters of absent crusaders. Boucicaut fought in the Battle of Agincourt, where he was taken prisoner, and probably died in prison in Yorkshire, England.

For a link to a website where can you read more about the incredible life of William Marshal, go to **www.usborne-quicklinks.com**

Legends of King Arthur

If there ever was a King Arthur, historians think he may have lived in the 5th century. But he probably wasn't called Arthur and, at that period, he certainly wouldn't have had strong stone castles or shining armor. Even so, legends of King Arthur and his Knights of the Round Table were extremely popular in medieval times.

Born to be king

Legends say that, long ago, Uther Pendragon, the King of England, fell in love with a duchess called Igraine. She was already married, but Uther was so desperate to marry her that he made a pact with Merlin the wizard. If Igraine could be his, he would give Merlin their first child. Uther got his wish, and the new queen gave birth to a boy - Arthur. As promised, Merlin whisked Arthur away, and Uther never heard of his son again. So, 16 years later, he died without a successor.

In this medieval painting, Igraine gives away Arthur to Merlin, as her husband has told her to. She doesn't know that it's the wizard because he's disguised as an old man.

This early medieval painting shows Arthur taking the sword out of the stone.

The sword in the stone

All this time, Arthur had been living in the court of Sir Ector, training to be a knight with Ector's son, Kay. One day, strange news came to the court. A stone had appeared in the yard of St. Paul's Cathedral in London, with a sword sticking out of it. On the sword were engraved the words: 'Whoever pulls this sword out of this stone is rightful king of all England.' All the knights in the country were invited to a tournament, to try their luck with the sword in the stone. Many powerful knights had already tried to pull it out, but all had failed.

Kay was to compete in the tournament - his first, as he had just been knighted. In his excitement he forgot his sword, and there was no time to go back and fetch it. So Arthur set off to try to find a sword - any sword - for Kay to use. When he spotted the sword in the stone, he didn't pause to think. He needed a sword fast and, with a sharp tug, he pulled it out. When everyone heard what he had done, they were amazed. How could this boy, a mere squire, possibly be the rightful king? But no one else was able to pull the sword out of the stone, and, a few days later, Arthur was crowned king of England.

The Round Table

With Arthur on the throne, everything began to take a turn for the better. The land was at peace for the first time in years, and Arthur fell in love with and married the beautiful Guinevere. But what would all Arthur's knights do now there were no wars to fight? Guinevere had the answer.

As a wedding present, Guinevere's father had given the couple a huge, round table, with room for Arthur and all his knights to sit around it. Arthur declared that, from now on, his knights would be known as the 'Knights of the Round Table.' They would spend their time riding off on adventures to help keep the peace - rescuing damsels in distress and challenging wicked knights to single combat. But, once a year, they would all return to court, to sit at the Round Table and recount their brave deeds.

Trouble and strife

The Round Table plan went well. Every now and then, one of Arthur's knights chopped off the wrong person's head by mistake, or was imprisoned by an evil enchanter, but mostly it came out alright in the end. Of all the Knights of the Round Table, Sir Lancelot was the one who never lost a fight or failed in a quest. He won admiration for his chivalry and bravery all over the land - and back at the court too.

Queen Guinevere found that she was in love with Lancelot. She met him in secret and discovered that he loved her too. They knew their love was wrong, but didn't know what they could do about it. To try to forget his feelings, Lancelot rode off on the most difficult quest of all - the quest for the Holy Grail.

In this 15th century painting, Mordred is shown wounding Arthur, while Arthur delivers a killing blow.

Arthur's death

While Lancelot was away, things went badly wrong for Arthur. Sir Mordred, a son Arthur had before he met Guinevere, arrived in court. He hated the queen, and kidnapped her. Arthur had no choice but to go to war against him. Knowing he had no hope of winning without Lancelot, Arthur sent for him. Lancelot set off as soon as he received the summons. But, by the time he arrived at the battlefield, it was too late. Just as he reached Arthur, he heard a horrible cry, as Mordred rushed at Arthur with a spear. As the spear struck him, Arthur brought his sword down with a mighty blow on his son's head. Mordred fell to the ground, dead, but he had already given Arthur a deadly wound.

Past and future king

According to some legends, Arthur died of that wound, and was buried with great honor in a marble tomb. Others say that Lancelot helped him to a boat that sailed away to a magic island, where the king was cured of his injuries. But all the stories agree that, when Britain needs him most, King Arthur will return.

Glossary

This glossary explains some of the words associated with knights and armor. If a word used in an entry has a separate entry of its own, it's shown in *italic* type.

A

arbalest A type of *crossbow*.

armet A type of helmet made from a skull-shaped piece, with added side pieces to cover the cheeks, and a *visor*.

arrow loop A slit in a wall through which soldiers fired arrows or guns.

aventail A *chain mail* neck protector.

B

bard A full suit of horse armor.

bascinet A rounded helmet, sometimes worn under a *great helm*.

battering ram A large log resting in a giant cradle that's swung back and forth to break down walls and doors.

battle-ax A metal-headed ax used for chopping at the enemy.

battlements Low walls on edge of the tops of walls and the roofs of towers.

beffroi *See belfry*

belfry A *siege tower*. Also known as a *beffroi*.

bird of prey A type of bird that hunts other animals for food.

blazoning Describing a *coat of arms*.

bolt An arrow fired by a *crossbow*.

bouche Groove in the top of a *tournament* shield to rest a *lance* in.

bracer Strap worn by an archer to protect his wrist while firing arrows.

bushido Strict moral code of the *samurai*.

C

caltrops Spiky weapons scattered on the battlefield to injure horses.

Cathar A *heretic* from the south of France.

cavalry The part of an army that fights on horseback.

chain mail Armor made from thousands of tiny metal rings linked together.

chivalry The code of conduct by which knights were supposed to live.

coats of arms Designs used to decorate shields and other parts of a knight's clothing and belongings. Originally used to identify armor-clad knights in battle.

coif A *chain mail* hood.

coronel A crown-shaped tip on a *jousting lance*, designed to lessen the impact and protect the competitors.

couching Holding a *lance* under the right arm to charge at the enemy.

courser A fast running horse used by knights.

couter Metal *plate armor* to protect the elbows.

crenel A gap in the tops of *battlements*.

crenellated Walls with gaps and solid parts along the top.

crinet Armor to protect a horse's neck.

crossbow A medium-range bow, the string of which had to be wound back.

cruppers Armor to protect a horse's flanks.

crusade A religious war.

D

daiymo A *samurai* warrior warlord.

destrier A knight's warhorse.

dubbing A light tap on the shoulders during the knighting ceremony.

E

enarmes A short leather strap which allows a knight to wear his shield on his left arm, leaving his right arm free to fight with.

F

falconry Hunting with *birds of prey*.

feudal system The way medieval society was organized: a system of rights and obligations based on land.

flail A metal bar or ball attached to a handle by a chain.

flanchards Armor to protect a horse's sides.

G

gambeson A padded garment worn under armor.

gauntlets Metal gloves or mittens to protect the hands.

great helm A cylinder-shaped helmet with straight sides and a flat, or slightly pointed, top.

greaves Leg armor.

guige A strap allowing you to sling a shield on your back.

H

halberd A long-handled weapon with a sharp blade, a spike and a hook.

harness A complete suit of *plate armor*.

hauberk A *chain mail* tunic.

heraldry The art of recognizing, designing and recording *coats of arms*.

heralds Men who study and memorize *coats of arms* and how to create them.

heretics People who held beliefs that were in conflict with the teachings of the Roman Catholic Church.

Holy Land An area in the Middle East, where Jesus Christ lived and died, including the city of Jerusalem.

Hospitallers A religious order of knights who fought in the *crusades*. Their full title was 'Knights of the Order of the Hospital of St. John.'

Hundred Years War A war fought between France and England between 1336 and about 1453.

I

infantry The part of an army that fights on foot.

interlude A short play sometimes staged between courses during a medieval feast.

J

jester A type of *minstrel* specializing in storytelling.

joust A type of competition at a *tournament* where knights ride at each other with *lances* and score points by hitting each other or knocking each other off their horses.

L

lance A heavy spear-like weapon used by knights to charge at their enemy with.

longbow A very powerful type of long-range bow used mainly by English and Welsh armies.

M

mace A club-like weapon with a short handle and heavy metal head for hitting the enemy.

machicolations Walkways that stuck out on the tops of castle and town walls. They had holes in them through which missiles could be dropped onto the enemy below.

mark of cadency A mark added to a family coat of arms by a son to create his own unique coat of arms.

mêlée A mock battle at a *tournament*.

merlons The solid parts of *battlements* that are *crenellated*.

merrills A board game rather like a complicated version of tic-tac-toe.

mews A building where hunting birds were kept.

minstrels Castle and court entertainers, including acrobats, musicians and storytellers.

moat Water-filled ditch surrounding a castle or town, to give it extra protection.

Mongols Horse-riding warriors from central Asia.

N

naphtha A substance that easily burst into flames. It was used in missiles by Muslim fighters.

P

pagan A person who doesn't believe in the Christian God.

page A very young trainee knight. The first step towards becoming a knight.

paladins Warriors on horseback who fought for Charlemagne, King of the Franks. They are considered to be the forerunners of knights.

palfrey A horse used by a knight to carry him around.

parade armor Armor made purely for show, which gave little or no protection.

pas d'armes A type of *tournament* competition in which a knight challenges other knights to fight him in one-to-one combat.

pauldrons Metal *plate armor* to protect the shoulders.

People's Crusade A *crusade* involving thousands of ordinary people, who went off to fight in the *Holy Land* against the Muslim Turks.

peytral Armor to protect a horse's chest.

pike A long-handled weapon, similar to an extra-long spear, used by foot soldiers.

plate armor Armor made from solid metal plates riveted together.

poleyns Metal *plate armor* to protect the knees.

poleax A long-handled weapon with a blade and a spike on the end, used by foot soldiers for attacking mounted knights.

pursuivant A trainee *herald*.

Q

quintain A target used by *squires* when training to be a knight.

R

ransom A fee paid in return for the release of a knight who has been captured by the enemy.

regard Horse insurance given by some kings to their knights in case their horses were killed in battle.

S

sabatons Metal *plate armor* to protect the feet.

sacret A type of *bird of prey* used by knights for hunting.

sallet A light helmet with a rounded skull piece that swept down over the neck at the back.

samurai An elite warrior class of knights in Japan.

scabbard A sheaf to keep a sword or dagger in and to protect the blade.

scutage A fee paid by English knights to avoid having to fight for their lord or king.

Seljuk Turks Muslim rulers of the *Holy Land* during the First *Crusade*.

shaffron Armor used to protect a horse's face.

shogun The most important *samurai* warrior.

siege Trapping people inside a castle or town and waiting until they surrender.

siege tower A wooden tower, often built on site during a *siege*, to enable soldiers to reach the *battlements*. *See also belfry*

spangenhelm A type of early medieval helmet made by riveting pieces of metal together.

spurs Spikes worn on the heels to make a horse move faster.

squire A trainee knight. The next stage towards becoming a knight after being a *page*.

T

Templars An order of religious knights who fought in the *crusades*. The full name of their order was the 'Knights of the Order of the Temple.' They were persecuted and disbanded in 1310.

Teutonic knights An order of German knights, founded during the Third *Crusade*, who went on *crusades* against *pagan* peoples in eastern Europe.

tournament A series of competitions between knights involving fighting on horseback and on foot.

trapper A cloth covering used to protect horses during battles and *tournaments*.

trebuchet A giant catapult.

trencher A hard, stale piece of bread used as a plate by the poorer members of wealthy medieval households.

U

undermining Digging under the walls of a castle or fortress to make them collapse - a technique sometimes used during *sieges*.

V

vamplate A protective guard on a *lance* to protect the knight's hand.

ventail A *chain mail* face protector.

visor The part of a helmet that covers the face. Visors were sometimes detachable or hinged, so that they could be lifted away from the face to enable the knight to see better.

W

war hammer A stout stick with a heavy, hammer-shaped head, used in battle.

Wars of the Roses A 30-year struggle for power between rival families for the English throne.

windlass A mechanical device used to wind back the string of a *crossbow*.

Index

Acknowledgements

Every effort has been made to trace the copyright holders of the material in this book. If any rights have been omitted, the publishers offer to rectify this in any subsequent editions following notification. The publishers are grateful to the following organizations and individuals for their permission to reproduce material (t=top, m=middle, b=bottom, l=left, r=right): Cover © Dan Barba/Stock Connection Distribution/Alamy, (background) © Tim Lynch; **p1** Photolibrary.com; **p2** The Royal Armouries/HIP/TopFoto; **p3** The Art Archive/Bodleian Library Oxford Bodley 264 folio 161r; **p4** © Darama/CORBIS; **p6** (tl) The Art Archive/Bodleian Library Oxford Bodley 264 folio 161r, (ml) Paul Isemonger Lewis; **p7** © Tim Lynch; **p8-9** Dick Clark/Mayhem Photographics; **p8** (l) © The Board of Trustees of the Armouries, **p9** (tr) By permission of the British Library, Royal MS 10 E IV, f.74v; **p10** (tr) Hermitage, St. Petersburg, Russia/Bridgeman Art Library; **p11** (ml) The Art Archive/Biblioteca Nazionale Marciana Venice/Dagli Orti, (br) The Art Archive/Cathedral Treasury Aachen/Dagli Orti; **p12-13** (borders) By permission of the British Library Royal 14 E. III f.89; **p12** (tr) Bibliothèque Nationale, Paris, France/Bridgeman Art Library, (mr) By permission of the British Library Harley 4431 f.135, (bl) Biblioteca Monasterio del Escorial, Madrid, Spain, Giradon/Bridgeman Art Library, (bm) Bibliothèque Municipale, Castres, France, Giraudon/Bridgeman Art Library; **p13** (l) By permission of the British Library, Royal Add. 42130 f.170, (r) By permission of the British Library Royal 16 G.VI f.301v; **p14** © Doug Steley/Alamy; **p15** By permission of the British Library, Add. 22493 f.1; **p16** Dick Clark/Mayhem Photographic; **p19** By kind permission of the Trustees of the Wallace Collection, London; **p20** (t), (m) and (b) © The Board of Trustees of the Armouries, (br) By kind permission of the Trustees of the Wallace Collection, London; **p21** (t) © The Board of Trustees of the Armouries, (tm) © MUSEE DE L'ARMEE - PARIS, (bl) © Archivo Iconografico, S.A./CORBIS, (bm) © MUSEE DE L'ARMEE - PARIS, (br) photograph by Stephen Moncrieff, with thanks to David Edge; **p22** (l) Malcolm Group Events Limited, Herstmonceux Castle Medieval Festival; **p24-25** Photograph courtesy of Christian Fletcher; **p24** (br) © The Board of Trustees of the Armouries; **p26** Photograph courtesy of Christian H. Tobler and Jay Allen; **p27** (ml) By kind permission of the Trustees of the Wallace Collection, London, (r) © The Board of Trustees of the Armouries; **p28** (tr)© The Board of Trustees of the Armouries, (bl) English Heritage; **p29** © The Board of Trustees of the Armouries; **p30** (l) Photograph courtesy of Christian H. Tobler; **p32** © The Board of Trustees of the Armouries; **p33** © The Board of Trustees of the Armouries; **p34-45** Dick Clark/Mayhem Photographic; **p35** By permission of the British Library, Yates Thompson 35 f.90v; **p36** Paul Isemonger Lewis; **p41** (tl) By permission of the British Library, Harley 1319 f.18, (br) Musée Conde, Chantilly, France, Giraudon/Bridgeman Art Library; **p46** © Clive Hawkins; **p47** (t) By permission of the British Library, Add.38537 f.29; **p50-51** 20th Century Fox/The Kobal Collection; **p50** (tl) By permission of the British Library, Royal 16 G. VI f.404v; **p52** (tr) By permission of the British Library, Royal 20 C. VII f44.v, (bl) © David A. Barnes/Alamy; **p53** © Michael Nicholson/CORBIS; **p54** (tl) By permission of the British Library, MS. Add. 18866 f.135; **p55** (t) By permission of the British Library, Add. 42130 f.82, (b) Bibliothèque Nationale, Paris; **p56** (l) Werner Forman Archive/L J Anderson Collection, (r) © Thomas Hohenacker/imagebroker/Alamy; **p57** © BBC, Photograph by Mike Hogan/BBC Photo Library; **p58** © Tim Lynch; **p59** By permission of the British Library, Royal 2 B. VII f.198v; **p61** (bl) © The Art Archive/Biblioteca Nazionale Marciana Venice/Dagli Orti; **p65** (tr) The Art Archive/University Library Heidelberg/Dagli Orti, (bl) N & A Unwin/Spiderwoodimages, with thanks to the English Heritage Events Department and the falconers "Raphael Falconry"; **p66-67** © Clive Hawkins; **p67** (br) Bibliothèque Nationale, Paris, France, Paris; **p68** The Art Archive/Bibliothèque Municipale Dijon/Dagli Orti; **p69** By permission of the British Library, Harley 4431 f.98v; **p70** (tr) akg-images/VISIOARS, (bl) By permission of the British Library, Harley 4431 f.145; **p71** (t) Bibliothèque Nationale, Paris, France/Bridgeman Art Library, (br) By permission of the British Library, Royal 2 A. XXII f.220; **p72** (b) By permission of the British Library, Cotton Nero E. II pt.1 f.130; **p73** (tl) © Gianni Dagli Orti/Corbis, (br) akg-images/British Library; **p74-75** © National Gallery Collection; By kind permission of the Trustees of the National Gallery, London/CORBIS; **p75** (tl) British Museum, London/Bridgeman Art Library; **p76** The Art Archive/Biblioteca Nazionale Marciana Venice/Dagli Orti; **p77** (tl) akg-images/Erich Lessing, (br) Hamburger Kunsthalle, Hamburg, Germany/Bridgeman Art Library; **p78-79** © Tim Krieger/Alamy; **p78** (bl) © Time Machine AG, photographer John Howe; **p79** (bl) The Art Archive/Bibliothèque Municipale Rouen/Dagli Orti; **p80** Paul Isemonger Lewis; **p81** By permission of the British Library, Lansdowne 1179 f.34v; **p82** (tl) Musée de la Tapisserie, Bayeux, France, With special authorization of the city of Bayeux/Bridgeman Art Library, (br) By permission of the British Library, Royal 20 A. II f.9; **p83** (tl) Bibliothèque Nationale, Paris, France/Bridgeman Art Library; **p84** (b) British Museum, London, UK/Bridgeman Art Library; **p85** (tl) Musée Dobree, Nantes, France, Giraudon/Bridgeman Art Library, (br) Phillips, The International Fine Art Auctioneers, UK, © Bonhams, London, UK/Bridgeman Art Library; **p86** By permission of the British Library, Cotton Claudius D. VI F.9v; **p87** By permission of the British Library, Cotton Nero E. II pt.2 f.220v; **p88** (bl) By permission of the British Library, Add. 10292 f.97v, (tr) By permission of the British Library, Add. 10292 f.101; **p89** (tr) By permission of the British Library, Royal 14 E. V f.439v

Art director: Mary Cartwright. Digital imaging: John Russell. Additional illustrations: Peter Dennis and Stephen Moncrieff. Picture Research: Ruth King. Cartographic Consultant: Craig Asquith.